Gluten Free Mama's Best Baking Recipes

"The PROOF is in the taste!"

Over 100 recipes that are Gluten Free and Wheat Free

This book was designed to be nourishing food for the body, soul and spirit.

"Beloved, I pray that you may prosper in all things and be in health just as your soul prospers.
3 John 2

By: Rachel Carlyle-Gauthier and Billie McCrea

Gluten Free Mama's Best Baking Recipes
"The Proof is in the Taste!" Over 100 Recipes that are Gluten Free and Wheat Free
by Rachel Carlyle-Gauthier & Billie McCrea

Printed in the United States of America

ISBN 978-1-60266-409-8

www.xulonpress.com

Dedication

To my daughter Lexie,
for you are my inspiration
for writing this cookbook
and designing these flour blends.
I am so thankful that you are
healthy and thriving.
Mommy Loves You!

AND

To my LORD in heaven,
for blessing me with
the gift and joy for cooking.

Rachel Carlyle-Gauthier

To the Lord,
without whose wisdom and direction
this cookbook
would not have been completed.

Billie McCrea

Table of Contents

"So shall My word be that goes forth from my mouth;
It shall not return to me void,
But it shall accomplish what I please,
And it shall prosper in the thing for which I sent it.
Isaiah 55:11

Introduction

My entire life, I have put my health and the health of my children into the hands of doctors. If they gave me a pill to take, I would take it. If they asked me to try different things, I would do it. I never really questioned it until the birth of my third daughter, Lexie. Slowly, my views of doctors began to change, and I learned how crucial it is to be pro-active in my health care and my children's health care.

Lexie was not an easy baby. She would scream from the moment she woke up until naptime, then after naptime she screamed until she went to bed at night. Nothing I did consoled her. I took several trips to the doctor, and he would just smile and say "some babies are just colicky." He would give me tips on calming her down, but nothing worked. Her dad was the only one who could comfort her. He would walk up and down the street holding her upright facing away from his chest, while he patted her back. She had enormous amounts of gas on both ends. Her stools were extremely loose.

Colic usually lasts about 6 weeks in babies. Six weeks came and went; the screaming continued. As the days passed, I had feelings of giving up. I even had horrible thoughts, of which I am deeply ashamed, of leaving her with the doctor and saying "well if you think it's so easy, you take care of her!" Thankfully, I had a little self-control left and the good sense not to do that.

Around 7 months, we began introducing cheerios, or small fish crackers in addition to regular baby food. When Lexie held the snacks in her hands her cheeks would suddenly get red. Soon after introducing food she began to get chronic diarrhea with severe rashes on her bottom. I started to get concerned. When I mentioned it to the doctor, he thought maybe she was allergic to the coloring in the crackers. So I stopped giving her the cheese crackers. Around 10 months, I stopped nursing and put Lexie on formula. BIG MISTAKE! She became even more sick.

Eventually, after yet another doctor visit, I recapped the last few months (the rashes, diarrhea, screaming) and the doctor suggested not feeding her wheat. So we accepted the idea hoping we would obtain some relief. This helped a little, but she was still reacting. Wheat seemed to be hidden in so many foods and every time I turned around she was getting exposed. When I would be baking cookies in my kitchen her face would get red and flushed from the flour that was airborne from the mixer.

Lexie continued to have chronic diarrhea and then began vomiting every night as soon as she would lie down for bed. When I had taken her to the doctor, I felt that I was being treated as an over-reactive mom. The doctor insisted it was a virus. I finally just broke down. I insisted that something more serious was wrong. I mentioned to the doctor that the ER doctor the night before suggested Celiac disease. I insisted they order the tests for Celiac Sprue, gluten intolerance, and allergies.

Introduction

Lexie's initial blood work did indicate possible celiac disease. The doctor consulted a GI who ordered a different test. This test came out normal; however, she had been off wheat for some time when taking this test. I questioned its accuracy, but the doctor insisted it was fine and that she was probably just allergic or had a virus. Her regular doctor concurred, and said just keep her away from wheat. We had the celiac disease scope of the intestine done, but it turned out negative, which we were thankful for.

Lexie just wasn't getting better. It broke my heart every time I had to change her diaper. She was having diarrhea almost every half hour. I finally had to do something, so I tried a Naturopath. This doctor was amazing, she agreed with me that something wasn't right, she acknowledged my feelings, and she praised me for being determined to get to the bottom of this. She put Lexie on some digestive enzymes, different homeopathic meds, high potency powder and L-glutamine powder. She also put her on goat's milk instead of cow's milk. She said that Lexie's gut was damaged and really needed to heal.

Lexie falls into the category of being gluten intolerant, allergic to soy, and cow's milk intolerant. What upsets me is that the doctors never suggested food could be the culprit in the beginning and didn't investigate until I demanded it. If I would have known that the food I was eating was coming through my breast milk and making her sick, I would have changed my diet, or found other means of feeding her. It upsets me that simple nutrition and diet caused my daughter and I misery for 20 months before it was even brought to my attention. Even then it was not doctors who brought it to my attention. It was through word of mouth, friends, the naturopath and my own endless research.

Lexie now strictly follows the gluten free diet. I have eliminated wheat flour in my house, and only use GF flours in baking now. We prepare all our family meals at home gluten free so that Lexie doesn't feel differentiated from. The challenge of preparing gluten free meals is making food that my family will actually eat and enjoy.
I struggled with the gluten free choices because most of the recipes we tried lacked flavor and had a gritty texture.

I felt inspired to write my own cookbook. Since a teenager I dreamed of writing a cookbook, however, I never thought I would be writing a gluten free cookbook. I decided to make lemonade out of lemons! I am now dedicated to helping Lexie enjoy food like the rest of us, and making the gluten free lifestyle easier for families all across our country. I feel that the Lord helped me through this journey with Lexie's health and inspired me and equipped me with the joy of cooking. He has also blessed be with a very godly woman, Billie McCrea, to work side by side on this project. We have dedicated our cookbook and business to serving the Lord.

Introduction

This cookbook and the Gluten Free Mama website are aimed at helping others like me embrace the new lifestyle and make it rewarding. Just because you are gluten free doesn't mean you need to stop living, stop having fun and stop eating good food.

"It's not what you can't have, but what you can have!"

I hope you enjoy the cookbook.

"Making Gluten Free Living Tastier"
The Gluten Free Mama, AKA Rachel Carlyle-Gauthier

ACKNOWLEDGEMENT: I am not a doctor, nor do I claim to be. Any questions or concerns about the gluten free lifestyle should be discussed with your personal doctor or naturopath doctor. This cookbook is strictly here to help people enjoy great tasting gluten free food.

....

My interest and first hand knowledge in gluten free flours and mixes comes as a result of mixing gluten free flours for my mother who has Celiac Sprue. She would buy several different flours and have me mix them together to make a flour blend. Through her research she found that gluten free breads could only handle a single rise. So she purchased a special bread machine for baking gluten free breads that only allowed for one rise. But the breads always seemed to be dry and crumbly. For years she searched for good gluten free recipes and bread products such as hamburger buns or a good sandwich bread that would not fall apart. After seeing how difficult it was for her to maintain a gluten free diet, I felt there needed to be a way to make life easier and tastier for people who must eat a gluten free.

I met Rachel Gauthier through my rubber stamping club. After she discovered her daughter had a gluten intolerance, she began experimenting with gluten free baking. She often brought samples for us all to try at our monthly meetings and asked if I might be interested in being a 'tester' for the recipes she was creating for a cookbook. For several months I tested her recipes in my kitchen, offering suggestions and full reviews as well as creating recipes myself. Rachel had designed two very tasty flour blends that not only made gluten free food taste better, but simplified the gluten free lifestyle by having only one mix to use rather than several flours. The project began to mushroom and she asked me to become a business partner. After prayer and consideration, Gluten Free Mama Kitchen, LLC was born.

We have created over 100 best tasting recipes from hamburger buns to sandwich bread, as well as tasty muffins, biscuits, cookies and more. Every recipe was tested in our kitchens and has been taste tested by several willing 'tasters' in our community. We hope that our recipes and flour blends give you the opportunity to start enjoying your food and enjoy living again.

Billie McCrea

Gluten Free Living Made Easier

GLUTEN FREE MAMA'S FLOUR BLENDS 101

Gluten Free Mama Kitchen (GFMK) has designed two perfectly formulated flour blends that will help simplify your gluten free baking; **Rice Almond Blend** and **Rice Coconut Blend**. Each blend contains the perfect combination of only the highest quality gluten free flours, assuring the best possible texture and flavor.

All of the recipes in this book are designed specifically to be used with these flour blends. Although some of the recipes may work with other flour blends, we cannot guarantee that they will produce the same quality, taste and texture. For the best results and optimum flavor choose our **Rice Almond Blend** or **Rice Coconut Blend.**

Our blends simplify the GF lifestyle. No need to buy 10 different flours and find storage for them in your kitchen. Now only one bag to buy and only one space in your cupboard taken. Baking becomes easier, too! Instead of measuring out 3 different flour for one recipe, all you need to do is replace the total GF flour amount with the same amount of **GFM's Rice Almond Blend** or **Rice Coconut Blend.**

Our blends are gluten free and processed in a certified gluten free facility. We also do Elisa testing to ensure the product meets gluten free standards.

Check our website often for new and upcoming blends, mixes and recipes. All of GFMK flour blends, mixes, aprons, and cookbooks can be purchased directly from our website.

Ask your local grocery store and health food store to carry Gluten Free Mama Flour Blends.

GLUTEN FREE MAMA FLOUR BLENDS 101

Gluten Free Mama's Rice Almond Blend is the perfect blend of only the highest quality gluten free flours that will optimize all your baked goods with a delicious flavor and texture. This blend is the best tasting and will bring incredible flavor to all your baked goods. Our **Rice Almond Blend** is high in fiber and protein and is the best choice for all your favorite recipes. You won't be able to tell that your baked goods are not made with wheat flour! The proof is in the taste!

Why do we use Almond Meal in our blend?
* Almond Meal offers superb flavor to GF baked goods.
* Almonds are high in nutritional value including: protein, fiber, folic acid, calcium, phosphorus and vitamin E.

What is the shelf life of GFM's Rice Almond Blend?
* The shelf life for this blend is 12 months.
* Extend the shelf life and freshness by storing in refrigerator or freezer.
* Store in a sealed airtight container for optimum freshness.

Can I use this blend in my favorite GF recipes?
* Absolutely! Replace the GF flour in your recipes with the same amount of any of GFM's Flour Blends.

What types of baked goods work best with the Rice Almond Blend?
* ALL of them. The **Rice Almond Blend** has been tested with every recipe in this cookbook and is our number one blend. It is completely versatile with any recipe.
* Especially offers the best flavor to pancakes, cookies and breads.
* In your favorite cake recipes, use this blend, however decrease the amount of flour by ¼-½ cup.

Do I need to use xanthan gum with this blend?
* Yes. Without xanthan gum your gluten free baked goods will crumble and fall apart. We do not add xanthan gum to our blends because each recipe requires different amounts of xanthan gum. Follow the recipe for how much xanthan gum to add.

Rice Coconut Blend

Gluten Free Mama's Rice Coconut Blend is the perfect blend of only the highest quality gluten free flours that will optimize all your baked goods with a delicious flavor and texture. **The Rice Coconut Blend** offers a unique "tangy" sweet taste and perfect texture to gluten free baking. This blend is high in fiber and protein. **Rice Coconut Blend** is best used in sweet breads, cookies, bars and cakes. Use this blend with a variety of GFM's recipes or try it with your favorite GF recipes.

Why do we use Coconut Flour in our blend?
* It is an excellent source of fiber and protein.
* It is low in digestible carbohydrates.
* It is a great alternative to wheat flour.
* It offers a unique tangy sweet flavor to your baked goods.

What is the shelf life of Rice Coconut Blend?
* The shelf life for this blend is 12 months.
* Extend the shelf life and freshness by storing in refrigerator or freezer.
* Store in a sealed airtight container for optimum freshness.

What types of baked goods work best with the Rice Coconut Blend?
* Breads, cookies, bars and cakes work best with this blend.
* Substitute with your favorite GF recipes cup for cup replacement.

Do I need to use xanthan gum with this blend?
* Yes. Without xanthan gum your gluten free baked goods will crumble and fall apart. We do not add xanthan gum to our blends because each recipe requires different amounts of xanthan gum. Follow the recipe for how much xanthan gum to add.

Gluten Free Living Made Easier

ORGANIZATION 101

The first step in making the "gluten free lifestyle" successful is organization! Cooking gluten free is a completely different science than cooking with traditional wheat flour. Getting started can be overwhelming, because now there are several different flours and new ingredients to incorporate in baking and learn how to use. Where do you begin? The best way to get started is by getting organized.

1. MINIMIZE

- **INVEST IN GLUTEN FREE MAMA FLOUR BLENDS AND MIXES**
  Gluten Free Mama flour blends are perfectly designed to work in all your everyday recipes. Eliminate the need for several different flours and invest in **GFM'S Rice Almond Blend** or **Rice Coconut Blend.** Look for GFM's mixes soon. You may order GFM's flour blends and mixes from our website at www.glutenfreemama.com. Look for them soon in health food stores near you.

- **MINIMIZE KITCHEN CLUTTER A clean kitchen is a fun kitchen to bake in.**

  * **Look through your cupboards and drawers and get rid of unnecessary items.** If you haven't used it in one to two years you probably don't need it. Who needs 20 different mugs? Choose three or four of your favorites.

  * **How much clutter do you have on your countertops?** Find a cabinet for rarely used appliances. Establish a junk drawer for mail, stickies, pens, box tops, etc.

  * **Is your pantry full of food you never eat?** Donate unused food to your local food pantry. Now that you are gluten free, minimize temptation by getting rid of all unsafe foods.

  * **How old are your spices?** How many duplicates do you have? Go through and throw away old spices. If they are older than 2 years they are outdated. And if they are in those tin containers they are outdated, unless it is pepper. Check for duplicates and combine.

  * **Do you know what is in your freezer?** Go through your freezer and start using up old items that you forgot about. This will help make room for a stock up of fresh baked GF foods to freeze for later.

ORGANIZATION 101

2. ORGANIZE GLUTEN FREE FLOURS AND BAKING GOODS

- **First designate a pantry shelf, or cupboard space exclusively for your gluten free flours and commonly used ingredients for baking.**
  * Include GFM's Flour Blends, xanthan gum, baking powder, baking soda, egg replacer (if used), honey, cider vinegar, vanilla, and etc.
  * Go to the local Wal-mart or Target and invest in some sturdy Rubbermaid containers in several different sizes. You will need at least 6.
  * GFM website had designed labels for you to label your containers. Print out labels and laminate them at the local UPS Store or Kinkos.
  * Go to your local health food store or shop www.glutenfreemama.com and order **GFM's Rice Almond Blend** and **GFM's Rice Coconut Blend Flours** and purchase your choice of GF flours that you intend to use. Sweet rice flour is a good GF flour to have on hand for coating cake pans and rolling out cookies. Xanthan gum is absolutely necessary for cooking GF, as it acts as a gluten and holds your baked goods together. Purchase a fresh container of yeast so that you can get started baking your choice of GFM's wonderful tasting breads.
  * Fill up your Rubbermaid containers with flours and stick your laminated labels onto the containers.
  * Stack your items nicely in your GF cupboard and now you are ready to start baking! You can see a picture of the Gluten Free Mama's cupboard by logging on to our website.

3. DESIGNATE A COOKBOOK FOR YOUR NEW GF RECIPES

All too often I will print out a new recipe off the internet that I want to try. Then what do I do with it after I try it? I throw it in the cupboard with food spills all stuck to it. Finally, one day after being disgusted with my disorganization, I designed a recipe card just for my GF recipes.

* Log onto www.glutenfreemama.com and print off recipe cards onto cardstock paper. Glue or tape your printed recipe onto the card.
* Purchase a 1 inch notebook and sheet protectors from your local office supply store. Place recipe cards into your sheet protector and insert into the notebook. Now your recipes will be protected from spills and organized in one spot!

ORGANIZATION 101

4. AN EFFICIENT KITCHEN

- **Designate Specific Areas for Baking Items**
  * Organizing your kitchen around the function of the kitchen will make baking much more efficient.
  * It is good to have your measuring cups, measuring spoons, rubber scraper, whisks and other essential baking items in a drawer close to your stand mixer. There is nothing worse than having to walk all the way across the kitchen just to get a clean rubber scraper.
  * Put hot pads, aluminum foil, spatulas, close to the oven, because that is where you will use these items most.

- **Hot Water in Sink**
  * Before getting started, always fill the sink with hot soapy water. That way if you need to quickly wash a measuring cup you can do it without much trouble. Also, it allows you to quickly soak dirty dishes and makes clean up more efficient.

- **Wear an Apron**
  Cooking is messy. I always get food on my clothes. I hate it when I accidentally spill or wipe my hands on my freshly washed pair of jeans. Wearing an apron is the best way to keep your clothes clean and avoid frustration. It also acts as a sanitation barrier between you and your food. You can order your own "Gluten Free Mama" apron at www.glutenfreemama.com.

BAKING BREAD 101

The number one complaint I get from those who live gluten free or who need to live gluten free is the fact they have to give up "real bread". It is true, eating bread will never be the same. Baking gluten free bread is a completely different science than traditional "wheat bread" baking. Traditional wheat breads have a key ingredient, GLUTEN, that allows the bread to become elastic when kneaded and helps to leaven the bread and make it have that perfect chewy texture. It is necessary to replace the gluten in GF breads with other products to make a good bread. Xanthan gum or guar gum are common substitutes for gluten to hold baked goods together and allow expansion. We can use other binders too like eggs, honey, molasses, and sweet rice. Adding eggs helps leaven the bread and gives it a chewy texture. Eggs also help to make the bread moist. We can also make the bread moist by adding butter, honey and molasses. Gluten Free Mama has taken GF bread to a higher level of excellence. After baking bread using our perfectly blended flour blends and recipes you will find yourself in love with bread again. We have formulated some tips below to help you bake bread more efficiently and perfect every time!

- **You need a good quality stand mixer to make GF bread.** GF bread dough looks more like a batter than a ball of dough. Therefore, it is necessary to beat the bread using a mixer on high speed versus traditional kneading. Beat your dough on high speed for at least 2 minutes. I like to beat mine for 3 minutes because it seems to give it more of an airy texture similar to regular bread.

- **The right consistency.** GF bread dough should be a smooth, thick batter. You should be able to easily run your rubber scraper across the batter to smooth it out. If you cannot do this, add 1-2 tablespoons of liquid. If the batter is too dry, your bread will turn out like a brick. Likewise, if your batter is too wet it will sink when baking. The more you bake bread the easier it will be to eyeball the correct consistency.

- **Measure ingredients accurately.** Use liquid measuring cups for liquid ingredients and dry measuring cups for dry ingredients. Don't pack the flour. See Measuring Tips 101 for more measuring guidelines.

- **Wet or dry dough.** Sometimes even with the best of measuring and following the recipe perfectly, you will still find that your dough is too wet or too dry. Sometimes eggs might be the culprit, depending on size or freshness, or the butter measurement might be off slightly or the flour was packed in a little more than usual. Whatever the reason, don't worry, just add 1-2 tablespoons extra GF flour to thicken the dough or an extra 1-2 tablespoons of liquid (water, milk, buttermilk) to moisten the batter.

BAKING BREAD 101

- **MUST ADD A GLUTEN REPLACEMENT:** Xanthan gum is derived from corn and is tasteless. It is the most commonly used replacement for gluten in GF baked goods. Guar gum is also tasteless and derived from beans. You may want to be careful how much guar gum you use as it is high in fiber and can act as a laxative if used in high amounts. All of GFM's recipes call for xanthan gum, however it is equally exchangeable with guar gum. Xanthan gum is expensive, however, it goes a long way.

- **Additional Binders.** In addition to xanthan gum and guar gum as a gluten replacement, GF breads need additional binders to improve texture and flavor, and to create a bread that is as close to wheat bread as possible. I like to use eggs, egg whites, honey, sweet rice, and sometimes molasses.

- **Use fresh yeast!** See Yeast 101 in this cookbook for tips about using yeast.

- **Yeast.** It is a good rule of thumb to use 1 tablespoon or one scant tablespoon of yeast for bread recipes that have 4 cups or less of flour. If making larger bread recipes, you can increase the yeast up to 2 tablespoons.

- **GF breads need moisture.** Buttermilk, yogurt, and cottage cheese are perfect ingredients that will help your bread to taste better and give it a wonderful springy and chewy texture. Be sure when using these ingredients, including milk, to bring them to room temperature before adding to the flour mixture. You can do this quickly by microwaving for 10-15 seconds or setting on your counter for at least ½ hour. Another quick tip is to fill a liquid measuring cup with water and microwave for 1-2 minutes. Remove from microwave and dump out water. Then measure out your buttermilk, yogurt or cottage cheese in the hot measuring cup.

- **Rising the bread.** Bread needs to have time to rise. Rise in a warm place in your kitchen until doubled in size. This process usually takes 1 to 1½ hours. Sometimes, I will turn the oven on the lowest temperature while mixing the dough and then turn it off and let my bread rise in the oven with the door cracked open. Cover the bread with a lightweight towel when rising so it doesn't dry out. Also, I recommend only doing a single rise. Due to the lack of gluten that wheat flour offers, GF breads cannot withstand a double rise.

- **GF breads generally need 50-60 minutes to bake.** To help prevent the crust from burning or becoming to crispy, cover the bread gently with foil without removing it from the oven after the first 20-30 minutes.

- **Oven Temperature.** Most of the bread recipes in this book are baked at 400°, however if using a glass loaf pan, reduce heat to 375°.

- **Softer crust.** Remove from pan after 20 minutes of cooling time. For a softer crust remove the bread from the loaf pan to a cooling rack after 10 minutes.

BAKING BREAD 101

- **Storing GF Bread.** Store bread in an airtight container for up to four days on the counter, or for one week in the refrigerator.

- **Use leftover bread.** GF bread is too expensive to waste. If you find that you can't use up your bread quick enough, make it into bread crumbs, croutons, melba toast or freeze it for later use. When freezing the bread, wrap it once with plastic wrap and then store it in an airtight, freezer safe, container for up to three months. To make bread crumbs, melba toast or croutons, follow the recipes in this cookbook.

TROUBLESHOOTING:

My dough didn't rise:

- **How much salt did you use?** Try decreasing the salt or increasing the salt by ¼ tsp. Salt should never come into direct contact with yeast, as it kills yeast. Mix salt in with the dry ingredients. If you live at low altitudes it may be a good idea to increase salt by ¼ tsp.

- **Did you use cold ingredients?** Be sure to bring eggs, milk, buttermilk, cottage cheese to room temperature before using. If it is too cold it will inhibit rising. Likewise if it is too hot it will inhibit rising. For milk and buttermilk you can speed up the process by microwaving for 10-15 seconds before using. Also you can set ingredients out on the counter for 30 minutes before using.

- **Was your yeast fresh and proofed properly?** Be sure to check your yeast's expiration date. If the yeast doesn't foam when combined with water after 5 minutes, then throw it out. Be sure to proof your yeast with warm water at 105°-115°. Water that is too hot or too cold will inhibit rising.

- **Did you beat the dough long enough?** Gluten Free bread dough needs to be beat on high speed for a minimum of 2 minutes; three minutes is best.

- **Was the batter to dry?** As a good rule of thumb you should be able to easily run a rubber scraper across your bread dough to smooth the surface for the best consistency and appearance. If you can't do this, the dough may be too dry. Add an additional 1-2 tablespoons of liquid.

Why did my bread sink after removing from oven.

- **Did you bake the bread long enough?** If the bread isn't thoroughly cooked it may sink after removing from oven. Bake bread for at least 50 minutes. Generally 55-60 minutes is best. Try increasing your time for your own oven the next time you try this recipe.

- **Was the batter too wet?** You want your batter to be somewhat wet, at least wet enough to run a rubber scraper through it. But if you dip your rubber scraper into the batter and it won't make the dough form peaks, then it is too wet. Add 1-2 tablespoons of flour to thicken it slightly.

BAKING BREAD 101

- **Did you allow the bread to rise properly?** Sometimes if you over rise the bread or rise it too fast in too warm of a spot it will cause the bread to sink. Be sure to rise your bread just until it doubles in size. Also, rise your dough at 80° or less. If my kitchen is too cold, sometimes I will turn on the oven for 5 minutes and then turn it off and let my bread rise in the oven with the door cracked. Or I will turn on the oven and let my bread set on top of the oven to reach the optimum rising temperature. In the summer a warm window is a good place to allow your bread to rise.

When slicing my bread it makes the knife too gummy.

- **Did you let the bread bake long enough?** Be sure to bake your bread according to recipe directions. If it isn't baked all the way it may cause the insides to be too moist and have a gummy texture.

- **Did you allow the bread to cool before cutting?** Unless otherwise stated in the recipe allow the bread to cool for at least 30 minutes before cutting.

My bread has a real rough texture on the crust.

- **Not enough moisture in the dough.** If your bread dough is too dry, the presentation of your crust will become hard, knotty, or present sharp crumbly edges.

- **Did you smooth out the top of the dough?** Gluten free bread dough looks like a thick batter. To make a good presentation on the finished product, it is important to use your rubber scraper and smooth out the top of the dough before rising.

REMEMBER: Gluten free baking takes a lot of patience. If you mess up on a loaf, don't let that keep you from trying again. PRACTICE MAKES PERFECT!

YEAST 101

What is Yeast?

Yeast is a single celled living organism that is used as a leavening agent in baking, particularly in breads. When combined with water and sugar it starts the process of fermentation, producing alcohol and carbon monoxide causing bread to rise. Bakers Yeast, AKA Active Dry Yeast, is what we use in baking. It is made up of dehydrated granules that are dormant. When these granules are mixed with warm water (105°-115°), the yeast becomes active. There is also Rapid Rise Yeast which can be mixed directly with dry ingredients without dissolving it in water. It takes half the time for the rising process as does regular active dry yeast. For better reliability in gluten free baking, GFMK recommends that you use regular active dry yeast with all our recipes. There are some important facts to know when working with yeast; see below.

FACTS:

Proof the yeast to check for optimum freshness.

* Add yeast to about ¼ cup water with a teaspoon of sugar. Set aside. If yeast is fresh it will develop a foamy layer above the water. After 5 minutes, if there is no foamy layer, throw the yeast out; it is not fresh.

Yeast needs a proper environment to grow.

* Temperature should be between 105°-115° F.

* Use a instant read thermometer to check temperature.

* Or drop a few drops on the inside of your wrist, like you would with a baby's formula. If it feels warm it should be right. If it feels hot, try again with a little cooler water.

*Combining yeast, warm water, and sugar together activates the yeast and stimulates growth. Sugar helps to activate the yeast.

* Let yeast rest for a few minutes before adding it to dry ingredients. If yeast mixture doesn't foam, throw it out and start over with fresh yeast.

YEAST 101

Salt inhibits the growth of yeast.

* Do not add salt to the yeast mixture. It will kill the yeast. It is best to mix dry ingredients together and then slowly pour in foamy yeast mixture to the dry ingredients.
* If your bread isn't rising try adjusting the salt. Decrease or add ¼ tsp. Typically 1 tsp. is appropriate for traditional bread recipes, but in gluten free recipes it is not uncommon to only need ¾ tsp.

Buying Yeast.

* Yeast can be bought at your local grocer or health food store.
* It comes in 4 oz jars, or ¼ oz packets. At Costco it comes in large 2lb bags. At the health food stores, you can buy it by the ounce.

Storing Yeast.

* Store yeast in a dry, cool environment.
* Store bought yeast in packages have a freshness date, or "use by" date.
* You can also store yeast in the refrigerator, but it loses its freshness more quickly. If storing in the refrigerator be sure to allow it to come to room temperature before proofing it with your warm water and sugar.

KITCHEN UTENSILS 101

It is not required to go out and buy all of the best kitchen utensils before you can begin baking Gluten Free (GF) foods. In fact, many kitchens will already have the basics covered. However, there are some important kitchen items that each kitchen needs or should consider investing in a little at a time that will make GF baking easier. Gluten Free Mama Kitchen (GFMK), has compiled a list that will hopefully help guide you for future buying decisions as well as make baking more efficient and easy. By all means, don't let the lack of any of these items keep you from baking! If you are new to the gluten free lifestyle or an old-pro it is important to remember that following the GF diet is the most important step to becoming healthy. Taking one day at a time is the only way avoid overwhelming yourself and giving up all together. Just remember one day at a time!

Essential Kitchen Items for GF Baking:

* **KitchenAid Mixer or a Good Quality Stand Mixer:** A good quality KitchenAid mixer is highly recommended if you plan to bake bread. It is the best quality on the market and will last forever. I have had mine for 15 years and I use it everyday, and I couldn't imagine life without it. When baking gluten free bread, it is important to beat the dough at high speed for nearly 3 minutes. It is important to have a good quality mixer that can withstand lots of wear and tear. If you have a good stand mixer don't feel like you need to rush out to the store and buy a Kitchenaid. A good quality stand mixer will work fine. Hand mixers are not recommended because they cannot withstand too much wear and tear. The motors burn out easily and by the time you replace three or four hand mixers, you may as well have bought a good stand mixer.

* **Measuring Spoons:** At least one good quality set of measuring spoons is recommended. I like to have two or three because I am usually baking two or three things, one right after the other, and I don't like to stop to do dishes. Choose a set of spoons that feel comfortable in your hand and that are easy to clean. A simple metal set from a discount store will work great.

* **Two Glass Liquid Measuring Cups:** It is important to have two sets when baking bread, one to measure out and proof the yeast mixture and one to measure out the remaining liquid ingredients. Pyrex is affordable and easily available.

* **Two Sets of Dry Measuring Cups:** Two sets are important if you do a lot of baking. If you are in the middle of the recipe and the one cup measure is dirty, you won't have to stop to wash the dishes if you have an extra set. Two basic plastic sets work great and are affordable.

KITCHEN UTENSILS 101

* **Rubber Scrapers:** Rubber scrapers in America are often called spatulas, however, the accurate name is rubber scrapers. Rubber scrapers are essential for measuring out dry ingredients, scraping the sides of mixing bowls, and smoothing out the batter of your homemade breads, muffins, pizza crusts, cakes and more. When looking for a rubber scraper, invest in a good quality one that will stand up to heat and wear and tear. KitchenAid has good quality silicone scrapers, the tops come off so you can clean up inside them which is very handy. Silicone scrapers are an excellent choice when scraping hot ingredients such as melted chocolate or butter. They can withstand temperatures of 500-600ºF.
* **Good Bread Pans:** Pyrex sells a 4 x 8 size glass loaf pan, and there are also brands like Baker's Secret that have metal pans that are 5 x 9. It is essential to have at least one good bread pan if you are going to bake bread. Gluten Free Mama has over 20 great bread recipes, so don't miss out!
* **Insulated Cookie Sheets:** There is debate about whether to use insulated Airbake type cookie sheets or regular non-stick metal pans. Opinions vary just as opinions as to whose chocolate chip cookie is the best. Just try them both out and see which you prefer. Airbake cookies sheets cause cookies to spread more. However, I think they are best for sugar cookies. Airbake cookie sheets also produce a softer, more evenly baked cookie versus one that has dark brown edges and not so baked center.
* **Cooling Racks:** Cooling racks are great options for cooling your muffins, cookies breads, rolls and etc. They allow the entire baked good to cool evenly. You can cool your baked goods without these and still have a good product. I often will line my countertop with paper towels and cool my cookies on the paper towels. Paper towels soak up unneeded grease!

Not So Essential Baking Items, But Fun To Have:

* **Garlic Press:** Garlic presses make mincing garlic fast, efficient and fun! Pampered Chef makes an excellent garlic press.
* **Basting Brush:** A good pastry brush is good for spreading cream on your scones before you bake them, sauce on your pizza crust or olive oil on your bread sticks. You can also purchase silicone brushes for spreading hot ingredients.
* **Food Chopper:** Any food chopper you can find that has rotating blades will work great for dicing, chopping, mincing nearly any vegetable, nut or herb during your baking. It makes chopping fun, easy and quick! Look for a food chopper that is easily cleaned or dishwasher safe.
* **Salad Shooter:** This is not an item you will use too much in baking but a lot in cooking main meals. It perfectly shreds or slices carrots, potatoes, zucchini, lettuce, cabbage, cheese, onions and more. I love it for making a quick batch of the Zucchini Fritters or Potato Pancakes in this cookbook!
* **Good Set of Mixing Bowls:** Glass mixing bowls that come in different sizes that stack nicely inside each other are also good items to have. They take up less room and come in handy for breaking eggs, melting butter and measuring out dry ingredients for cookies and breads.
* **Vegetable Peeler:** The best one ever is from Pampered Chef. It simplifies peeling potatoes and carrots and never dulls!

WEIGHTS AND MEASURES-CONVERSIONS 101

When creating new recipes and converting your favorite recipes to gluten free, you often need to alter the amount of flour or liquid ingredients to make the perfect chemistry. This useful conversion chart will help you make accurate measurements.

*** tsp. = teaspoon * Tbsp. = tablespoon * lb. = pound *oz. = ounce**

3 tsp.	=	1 Tbsp.
4 Tbsp.	=	¼ cup
5⅓ Tbsp.	=	⅓ cup
8 Tbsp.	=	½ cup
10⅔ Tbsp.	=	⅔ cup
12 Tbsp.	=	¾ cup
16 Tbsp.	=	1 cup

1 cup	=	8 fluid ounces
2 cups	=	1 Pint
4 cups	=	1 Quart
2 pints	=	1 Quart
¼ lb.	=	125 Grams
½ lb.	=	250 Grams
1 lb.	=	500 Grams

MEASURING TECHNIQUES 101

When baking gluten free recipes in this cookbook, it is imperative to make accurate measurements to produce the best results. Here are some tips that will help you be successful when making your baked goods.

* **Measuring Spoons**– When measuring out dry ingredients such as spices, baking powder, baking soda, salt, etc., dip the spoon into the dry ingredient and level off with a rubber scraper or flat side of a knife across the top of the spoon. When measuring sticky or wet ingredients such as peanut butter, butter, honey, etc., fill the same way, but be careful to remove the portions that stick to the underside of the spoons before adding the ingredient to your mixing bowl.

* **Dry Measuring Cups** -- When measuring dry ingredients, always use dry measuring cups. They can be found in plastic or metal in the kitchen section at your local discount store. Measuring gluten free flours is different than regular wheat flour. Start by scooping the flour into the measuring cup. Take the back of a rubber scraper and gently tap the top rim of the measuring cup to help settle the flour and remove air holes. Add more flour as necessary and repeat. Use the back of the rubber scraper and scrape from one side of the cup to the other making a level scoop. With all dry ingredients be sure to scrape the top rim making a level scoop for the most accuracy in baking. Do not pack the flour.

* **Liquid Measuring Cups** – Always use liquid measuring cups when measuring liquid ingredients such as oil, water, milk, etc. They can be found in glass or plastic in the kitchen section at your local discount store. Pyrex is the best brand to use because it is microwave safe and affordable. On the sides of the liquid measuring cups are measurements from ¼ cup-2 cups. Pour the desired amount of the liquid ingredient into the measuring cup. Set the measuring cup on a level surface like a counter and look at the measurement at eye level. The liquid should be exactly on the line, not under or over. Add or take away as needed and double check to ensure the accuracy of your measurement.

MORE GLUTEN FREE MAMA TIPS

Why is there a picture of a camera on some of the recipes?

* The camera symbolizes that you can view a picture of this recipe on our website. Log on to www.glutenfreemama.com to see pictures.

Should I use Vanilla Extract or Imitation Vanilla?

* It is best to use "pure" vanilla extract. Pure vanilla extract is derived from vanilla beans and has the best flavor.
* Imitation Vanilla is derived from synthetic substances made to imitate the flavor and smell of pure vanilla. When offered a choice natural ingredients are always better than synthetic.

What oven rack should I use?

The newer ovens have 7 racks to choose from, where the older ovens have 5 or less. The general rule of thumb is for baked goods that bake for an hour or longer are placed on a lower rack; baked goods that bake 30-45 minutes can be baked on center rack; baked goods that bake 15 minutes or less bake on an upper rack.

* For breads that bake 50 minutes or longer, bake on second rack from the bottom.
* For cookies, brownies and bars, bake on center rack.
* For biscuits, rolls and pizza crusts, bake on rack just above the center rack, or one of the upper racks.
* For pies crusts bake on an upper rack.
* For filled pies bake on second rack from bottom.
* For crackers bake on rack just above center rack.

Should I buy salted butter or unsalted butter?

* The recipes in this cookbook were created using regular salted butter. If you choose to use unsalted butter, you may want to increase the salt slightly in the recipe.

Should I use white sugar, natural cane sugar or turbinado?

* This question is ultimately decided by the consumer. See descriptions below. They all can be used as a cup for cup replacement.
  — **White Sugar**... White sugar is stripped of all its nutritional value and natural flavor during processing. It is 99% sucrose.
  — **Natural Cane Sugar** (Unrefined Cane Sugar)...This sugar is light brown in color and similar in texture to white sugar, but without the chemical refining. Natural cane sugar is evaporated fresh squeezed cane juice, and is produced from the first crystallization. This process preserves sugars natural flavor and nutrients.
  — **Turbinado Sugar (Raw Cane Sugar)** Turbinado sugar is light brown crystals of sugar that have not had the molasses or nutrients removed from them. It has a molasses or honey like taste to it. It is a coarse sugar and great for sprinkling on scones, muffins, and other desserts.

MORE GLUTEN FREE MAMA TIPS

EGG SUBSTITUTIONS

If I am allergic or intolerant to eggs can I still use the recipes in this cookbook?

* Yes. There are egg substitutes that you can use.
  - — **Ener-G egg replacer**. Ener-G egg replace can be purchased at most health food stores. Follow the instructions on box for use.
  - — The Food Allergy & Anaphylaxis Network has some excellent sources for egg replacement. (Courtesy of The Food Allergy & Anaphylaxis Network, www.foodallergy.org/allergens/egg.html. Provided with permission.)

    * 1 tsp. baking powder, 1 Tbsp. liquid, 1 Tbsp. vinegar
    * 1 tsp. yeast dissolved in ¼ cup warm water
    * 1½ Tbsp. water, 1½ Tbsp. oil, 1 tsp. baking powder
    * 1 packet gelatin, 2 T. warm water. Do not mix until ready to use.

  - — **Recipezaar has a great suggestion for egg replacer.** (Courtesy of Recipezaar www.recipezaar.com/library/getentry.zsp?id=424 Provided with permission)

    *1 tablespoon ground flaxseeds and 3 tablespoons water

    Simmer flaxseeds and water in a saucepan for 5 minutes (more or less time depending on the amount you are making) until a thick, egg-like consistency has been reached. Let cool before using in a recipe. Makes 1 egg's worth (can be doubled or tripled), and will keep in the refrigerator for about 2 weeks. Use about ¼ cup (which is equal to 4Tbsp) egg substitute for every egg.

* **Note:** None of the recipes in this book have been tested using these egg replacements. We have listed these suggestions as a courtesy to our readers.

Are oats gluten free?

* Gluten Free is described as being free of wheat, barley, rye and sometimes oats. Oats has been the topic of debate among the gluten free consumers. Some companies now make Certified Gluten Free Oats that test at less than 10ppm of gluten. The national standard for GF is less than 20ppm. Certified Gluten Free Oats are grown by dedicated growers that ensure no cross contamination and they manufacture the oats in gluten free facilities. If you have not had oats in your diet, you should introduce them slowly to see how your body responds. If you are unsure about introducing gluten free oats into your diet, check with your physician first.

Can the recipes calling for milk be substituted with non-dairy alternatives?

* Yes, most of the recipes in this cookbook that call for milk can be substituted using Lactaid, goat milk, rice milk and soy milk. Exchange cup for cup.

Breads

*"And Jesus said unto them, 'I am the Bread of Life.
He who comes to me shall never hunger;
and he who believes in me shall never thirst."
John 6:35*

Apple Walnut Bread

Ingredients:

1⅔ cups **GFM's Rice Almond Blend Flour**
1 tsp. cinnamon
⅛ tsp. cloves
¼ tsp. nutmeg
½ tsp. salt
½ tsp. baking soda
1½ tsp. baking powder
1½ tsp. xanthan gum
½ tsp. fresh lemon zest
½ cup walnuts, chopped

2 eggs
1 tsp. vanilla
⅓ cup canola oil
¼ cup brown sugar, packed
¾ cup sugar
1½ cups apple pieces, diced
2 Tbsp. sugar (for dusting)

GFM Tip:
This bread is great served with Apple Butter!

Directions:

Preheat oven to 350°. In a medium bowl combine flour, cinnamon, cloves, nutmeg, salt, baking soda, baking powder, xanthan gum, lemon peel and walnuts. Mix lightly until combined and set aside.

In a stand mixer combine eggs, vanilla, oil, brown sugar, sugar and apple pieces. Mix on medium speed for 30 seconds until well combined. Add dry ingredients and mix on low speed just until combined. Do not over mix!

Spray one 4 x 8 loaf bread pan with non-stick oil spray and pour bread batter into loaf pan. Smooth top evenly with a spatula and lightly sprinkle with sugar.

Place bread on second lowest rack in preheated 350° oven. Bake for 30 minutes and then without removing bread from oven cover with foil and bake 25-30 minutes more for a total baking time of 1 hour. Foil prevents over browning.

Test for doneness with a clean dry knife inserted in the center. If knife looks wet, bake an additional 5 minutes. If knife appears dry, bread is done. Remove from pan and cool on a cooling rack for 30 minutes before slicing.

"He sent His Word and healed them, and delivered them from their destructions."
Psalm 107:20

Banana Coconut Bread

Ingredients:

2 cups **GFM's Rice Coconut Blend Flour**
1½ tsp. baking soda
1 tsp. salt
2 tsp. xanthan gum

1 cup butter, room temperature
1¼ cups sugar
2 eggs
2 tsp. vanilla
2 large bananas, mashed
½ cup buttermilk

½ cup shredded coconut
½ cup chopped walnuts

GFM Tip: Try using pecans in place of the walnuts for a different taste.

Directions:

Preheat oven to 325°. Spray 4 x 8 bread pan with non-stick cooking spray. In a medium bowl combine flour, baking soda, salt and xanthan gum. Whisk lightly with a fork to combine. Set aside.

In a stand mixer cream butter and sugar for 1 minute. With mixer running on low speed, add eggs one at a time. Stop mixer and add mashed bananas, vanilla and half of buttermilk. Beat on high speed for 1 minute. Pour half of flour mixture into wet ingredients. Mix on low speed until mixed in. Repeat with remaining flour. Mix for another 30 seconds. Stir in coconut and walnuts and mix until well combined, about 30 seconds longer.

Pour batter into prepared bread pan. Place bread on second or third rack from bottom in preheated 325° oven. Bake for 20 minutes and then without removing from oven cover with foil and bake for an addition 60-65 minutes, for a total baking time of 1 hour 20 minutes. Allow to cool completely before slicing.

Note: This recipe also tastes great with **GFM's Rice Almond Blend Flour.**

"But the LORD is faithful who will establish you and guard you from the evil one."
2 Thessalonians 3:3

Banana Poppy Seed Bread

Ingredients:

½ cup margarine
1 cup sugar
2 eggs
3 extra ripe bananas
2 tsp. vanilla
1 tsp. lemon juice

2¼ cups **GFM's Rice Almond Blend Flour**
2 tsp. xanthan gum
2 tsp. baking powder
1 tsp. baking soda
½ salt
¼ tsp. cinnamon
¼ cup poppy seeds

GFM Tip: Check for sales where grocers often bag and sell ripe banana at a 75% discount. These bananas are great for baking.

Directions:

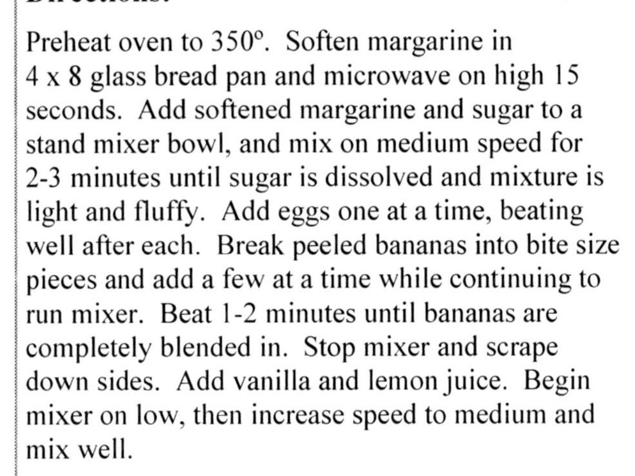

Preheat oven to 350°. Soften margarine in 4 x 8 glass bread pan and microwave on high 15 seconds. Add softened margarine and sugar to a stand mixer bowl, and mix on medium speed for 2-3 minutes until sugar is dissolved and mixture is light and fluffy. Add eggs one at a time, beating well after each. Break peeled bananas into bite size pieces and add a few at a time while continuing to run mixer. Beat 1-2 minutes until bananas are completely blended in. Stop mixer and scrape down sides. Add vanilla and lemon juice. Begin mixer on low, then increase speed to medium and mix well.

Combine flour, xanthan gum, baking powder, baking soda, salt, cinnamon, and poppy seeds in a separate bowl and whisk together until well blended. Add all at once to wet ingredients in mixer bowl. Mix on low speed until dry ingredients are mixed in. Stop mixer and scrape down sides. Beat on high speed 3 minutes.

Spray 4 x 8 glass bread pan (that was used to soften margarine) with oil pan spray. Pour banana bread batter into pan. It should flow easily. Place on lowest oven rack. Bake for 35 minutes, then without removing from oven, quickly lay foil over top and continue baking for 25 minutes, for a total of 1 hour. If center needs additional time, uncover and bake 5-10 minutes longer. Remove pan from oven and allow bread to cool in pan for 15 minutes. Remove bread from the pan to a cooling rack.

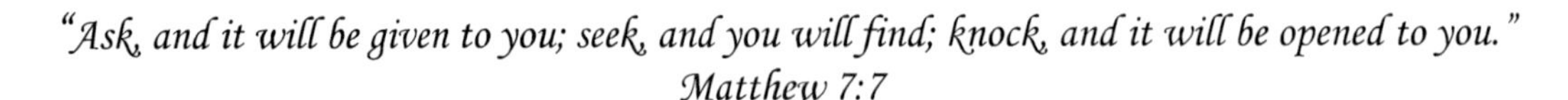

"Ask, and it will be given to you; seek, and you will find; knock, and it will be opened to you."
Matthew 7:7

Best Ever Corn Bread

Ingredients:

¾ cup **GFM's Rice Almond Blend Flour**
1 cup cornmeal
⅓ cup sugar
2 tsp. baking powder
1 tsp. baking soda
1 tsp. salt
1½ tsp. xanthan gum

2 eggs
1 cup milk
2 Tbsp. honey

GFM Tip:
This cornbread is sure to be a winner at any chili feed. Your friends won't be able to tell that it is gluten free!

Directions:

Preheat oven to 400°. Lightly grease and flour 8 inch square pan. In a medium bowl combine flour, cornmeal, sugar, baking powder, baking soda, salt and xanthan gum. Stir with a fork to combine. Set aside.

In a stand mixer add eggs, milk and honey. Stir on low speed 20-30 seconds until eggs are combined. With mixer on low speed, slowly add flour mixture until all flour is combined with wet ingredients. Scrape down sides of bowl. Mix on low speed 20-30 seconds longer.

Evenly spread batter into a prepared 8 inch square pan. Smooth out top with rubber scraper. Bake in preheated 400° oven on center rack for 18-22 minutes or until top is golden brown and toothpick inserted in center comes out clean. For a softer crust, allow bread to remain in pan 5 minutes before removing to a cooling rack or waxed paper. Serve warm or cooled!

Serves: 8

"Great is the LORD, and greatly to be praised;
And His greatness is unsearchable."
Psalm 145:3

Cinnamon Raisin Bread

Ingredients:

¼ cup warm water (105°-115°)
1 Tbsp. yeast
2 Tbsp. sugar

3½ cups **GFM's Rice Almond Blend Flour**
1½ tsp. xanthan gum
1 tsp. salt

1 cup milk
½ cup sugar
¼ cup butter or margarine

1 egg
1 tsp. cider vinegar
1 cup raisins

Cinnamon Filling:
¼ cup sugar
1 tsp. cinnamon

1 Tbsp. butter or margarine

GFM Tip:
Try using a combination of golden raisins with regular raisins.

"Pray without ceasing."
1 Thessalonians 5:17

Directions:
Spray a 4 x 8 loaf pan with non-stick spray.
In a large liquid measuring cup combine warm water, yeast and sugar. Mix until yeast and sugar are dissolved. Set aside for 5 minutes until foamy.

In a stand mixer add flour, xanthan gum, and salt. Combine on low speed. In a small sauce pan add milk, sugar and butter cut in small pieces. Heat on medium low just until butter is melted. Do not boil. With mixer running on low, slowly pour yeast mixture into dry ingredients. Pour in milk mixture. Add egg and vinegar. Stop mixer, scrape sides of bowl and beat on high speed for 2 minutes. Fold in raisins by hand.

Spread half of bread dough evenly into prepared loaf pan. Combine cinnamon filling and sprinkle half of cinnamon sugar mixture across top evenly. Swirl with a knife through mixture. Gently shake bread pan to allow cinnamon sugar mixture to fall into swirls. Spread remaining dough on top. Evenly smooth top of dough with rubber scraper. Sprinkle with remaining cinnamon sugar mixture. Again, swirl your knife through top of dough. Gently shake pan to allow cinnamon sugar mixture to fall into swirls. Pinch remaining tablespoon of butter into small pieces and place evenly across top of bread dough. Let rise until dough reaches top of loaf pan or doubles in size, about one hour.

Preheat oven to 375°. Place bread on second lowest rack. Bake for 30 minutes and then without removing from oven cover bread with foil and bake for an additional 30 minutes, for a total baking time of 1 hour. Foil will prevent crust from burning. Cool for 20 minutes before slicing. Serve warm or cold.

Cottage Dill Bread

Ingredients:

½ cup warm water (105°-115°)
1 scant Tbsp. yeast
1 Tbsp. sugar

2¾ cups **GFM's Rice Almond Blend Flour**
1 tsp. salt
¼ tsp. baking soda
1½ tsp. xanthan gum
2 Tbsp. fresh dill
2-3 Tbsp. minced onion

1 cup small curd cottage cheese, room temp.
2 Tbsp. butter, melted
2 egg whites
2 Tbsp. honey
1 tsp. cider vinegar

GFM Tip:
If you don't have fresh dill, add 2 tsp. of dried dill instead.

Directions:

In a liquid measuring cup, stir warm water, yeast, and sugar until dissolved. Set aside until top is foamy, about 5 minutes.

In a stand mixer combine flour, salt, soda, xanthan gum, dill weed, and onion. Add yeast to dry ingredients and mix on low speed. Add cottage cheese, butter, egg whites, honey and vinegar. Stop mixer and scrape side of bowl. Mix on high speed 2-3 minutes.

Spread bread dough into a small 6 inch round baking dish, or a regular 4x8 inch loaf bread pan. Smooth out top with a buttered rubber scraper. Cover and let rise in a warm place for about an hour or until dough has doubled.

Drizzle or spritz melted butter over top of dough. Preheat oven to 375°. Place bread on 2nd lowest rack in oven. Bake for 30 minutes and then without removing from oven, cover with foil and bake an additional 30 minutes, for a total baking time of 1 hour. Foil prevents over browning. Allow bread to cool 20 minutes before slicing.

*"Teach me to do Your will, For You are my God;
Your spirit is good. Lead me in the land of uprightness."
Psalm 143:10*

Delightful Buttermilk Bread

Ingredients:

⅔ cup warm water (105°-115°)
1 scant Tbsp. yeast
1 Tbsp. sugar

3¼ cups **GFM's Rice Almond Blend Flour**
1½ tsp. xanthan gum
¾ tsp. salt

2 egg whites
2 Tbsp. melted butter or margarine
¾ cup buttermilk, room temperature
1 tsp. cider vinegar
2 Tbsp. honey

GFM Tip: To bring buttermilk to room temperature quickly: heat water in liquid measuring cup in microwave for 1 minute. Empty water and add buttermilk. Allow buttermilk to sit in cup while preparing other ingredients.

Directions:

Spray a 4 x 8 loaf bread pan with non-stick oil cooking spray.

In a liquid measuring cup, stir warm water, yeast, and sugar until dissolved. Set aside 5 minutes until top is foamy.

In a stand mixer bowl add flour, xanthan gum, and salt. Mix on low until combined. Separate egg whites. Place butter in a small glass bowl, cover with wax paper, and microwave 10 seconds to melt. With mixer on low speed add yeast water, egg whites, butter, buttermilk, vinegar and honey to dry ingredients. Stop mixer and scrape down sides of bowl. Mix on high speed for 3 minutes. Dough will look like a thick batter.

Spread dough evenly into prepared pan. Smooth top with a buttered spatula. Let dough rise to top of pan or until double in size, about 1 hour.

Preheat oven to 400°. Place bread on second lowest rack. Bake for 30 minutes and then cover with foil without removing from the oven, and continue baking for 25 minutes more, for a total baking time of 55 minutes. Remove from pan and let cool for 30 minutes before slicing.

Note: If using a glass bread pan, reduce oven temperature to 375°.

"And above all things have fervent love for one another, for love will cover a multitude of sins."
1 Peter 4:8

Double Chocolate Zucchini Bread

Ingredients:

3 cups **GFM's Rice Almond Blend Flour**
2 tsp. xanthan gum
1 tsp. salt
2 tsp. baking powder
½ tsp. baking soda
2 cup sugar
2 tsp. cinnamon
½ cup cocoa

2 cups zucchini, shredded
4 large eggs
1 cup oil
2 tsp. vanilla
1-2 cups chocolate chips

2 Tbsp. sugar

GFM Tip: Freeze 2 cup portions of grated zucchini in individual freezer bags for baking after summer harvest.

Directions:

Preheat oven to 350°. In large bowl combine flour, xanthan gum, salt, baking powder, baking soda, sugar, cinnamon and cocoa. Mix lightly until combined.

In a stand mixer bowl combine zucchini, eggs, oil and vanilla. Mix on medium speed for 1 minute. Add one third of dry ingredients, and mix on low speed just until combined. Repeat with remaining flour. Do not over mix. Add chocolate chips and mix just until combined.

Spray 2 loaf pans with canola spray. Pour half of batter into each pan. Lightly sprinkle tops of each bread with sugar. Bake in preheated 350 ° oven just below center rack for 1 hour or until knife inserted in middle comes out clean.

"For He Himself is our peace, who has made both one, and has broken down the middle wall of separation."
Ephesians 2:14

French Yogurt Bread

Ingredients:

⅔ cup warm water (105°-115°)
1 Tbsp. yeast
1 Tbsp. sugar

3 cups **GFM's Rice Almond Flour Blend**
1 ½ tsp. xanthan gum
1 tsp. salt

2 Tbsp. butter, melted
8 oz. GF vanilla or plain yogurt
2 Tbsp. honey
1 egg + 1 egg white
1 tsp. cider vinegar

GFM Tip: For a great presentation on the top of bread: After rising, gently take a sharp knife and make a slash through the top of the bread lengthwise, then do four slashes across the width.

Directions:

Spray 4 x 8 loaf pan with nonstick cooking spray. Stir together water, yeast and sugar. Set aside 5 minutes until foamy.

In a stand mixer add flour, xanthan gum, and salt. Mix on low speed to combine. With mixer on low speed add yeast mixture slowly to flour. Turn mixer off and add butter, yogurt, honey, egg, egg white and vinegar. Turn mixer on high speed and beat 2 minutes. Transfer dough to prepared loaf pan. Smooth out top of dough with rubber scraper for a good presentation after baking.

Allow bread dough to rise in a warm place for 1 to 1½ hours. The dough should rise to top of bread pan or slightly higher. Preheat oven to 375°. Place bread on second lowest rack in oven. Bake 30 minutes and without removing from oven cover with foil and then continue baking for 30 minutes, for at total baking time of 1 hour. Foil prevents bread from over browning. Allow bread to cool for 20 minutes before slicing.

"Man does not live by bread alone but on every word that comes from the mouth of God"
Matthew 4:4

Fry Bread

Ingredients:

Oil for frying

3 cups **GFM's Rice Almond Blend Flour**
1 tsp. xanthan gum
1 Tbsp. baking powder
1 tsp. salt
2 Tbsp. powdered milk
2 Tbsp. light brown sugar
1½ cups warm water

GFM Tip:
This recipe reminds me of elephant ears at the county fair!

Directions:

Preheat oil in deep fat fryer, or in fry pan on stove top, to 375°.

Combine flour, xanthan gum, baking powder, salt, powdered milk and sugar. Slowly add water. Dough should be workable with the hands, but not dry. Add more flour or milk as needed.

Using a 1½ inch scoop, portion out dough onto a very lightly floured counter. Lightly flour hands and press each ball of dough into a round, flat circle. Dough flattened to ⅛ inch will have a crisper texture than dough flattened to ¼ inch thickness, which will be thicker and more chewy. Place in preheat oil until each side is lightly browned. Remove from oil to paper towel lined plate.

Spread with butter and sprinkle with cinnamon sugar, or spread with butter and drizzle with honey.

"Enter into His gates with thanksgiving, and into His courts with praise.
Be thankful to Him, and bless His name."
Psalm 100:4

Garlic Onion Bread

Ingredients:

1¼ cups warm water (105°-115°)
1 Tbsp. sugar
1 Tbsp. yeast

3 cups **GFM's Rice Almond Blend Flour**
2½ tsp. xanthan gum
1 tsp. salt
2 Tbsp. instant powdered milk
¼ tsp. ground pepper
¼ cup dried minced onion
2 tsp. garlic, minced

1 egg
2 Tbsp. butter, melted
1 tsp. cider vinegar
2 Tbsp. honey

GFM Tip: For an authentic Italian presentation, bake in a French loaf pan and reduce baking temperature to 375°.

Directions:

Spray one 4x8 loaf pan with non-stick cooking spray. Stir warm water, sugar and yeast until dissolved. Set aside 5 minutes until foamy.

In a stand mixer bowl add flour, xanthan gum, salt, powdered milk, pepper, minced onion and garlic. Mix on low speed until combined.

Melt butter in glass bowl covered with waxed paper for 15 seconds in microwave. Add yeast mixture to dry ingredients and mix on low until combined. Add egg, melted butter, vinegar and honey. Mix on medium high speed for 2 minutes. Spread dough evenly in prepared loaf pan. Allow dough to rise 1 hour or until doubled in size.

Preheat oven to 400°. Place bread on second lowest rack in oven. Bake for 30 minutes and then cover with foil without removing from oven and bake 30 minutes more, for a total baking time of 1 hour. Foil will prevent over browning.

Allow bread to cool 20 minutes before slicing.

"...but we also glory in tribulations, knowing that tribulation produces perseverance, And perseverance, character, and character, hope."
Romans 5:3

Glazed Lemon Bread with Almonds

Ingredients:

2 cups **GFM's Rice Almond Blend Flour**
1½ tsp. baking powder
½ tsp. salt
1½ tsp. xanthan gum
1 Tbsp. fresh lemon zest

½ cup butter or margarine
1 cup sugar
2 eggs
2 Tbsp. fresh squeezed lemon juice
(about half a lemon)
1 cup milk

Glaze:
½ cup powdered sugar, sifted
1 Tbsp. lemon juice

¼ cup slivered almonds

GFM Tip:
For fresh lemon zest, grate entire lemon peel surface over grater before slicing and juicing lemon.

Directions:

Preheat oven to 350°. In a medium bowl combine flour, baking powder, salt, xanthan gum and lemon zest. Whisk lightly with a fork and set aside.

In stand mixer, beat butter for 1 minute until light and fluffy. Add sugar and beat for 30 seconds. Add eggs, fresh lemon juice and milk. Beat for 30 seconds until well combined. Pour half of flour mixture into wet ingredients and mix on lowest speed for 10 seconds. Add remaining flour and stir on lowest speed for 30 seconds until well combined. Don't over beat.

Pour batter into greased 8 x 8 cake pan. Bake in 350° oven for 40-45 minutes or until top bounces back when touched and toothpick inserted in center comes out clean. Allow bread to cool in pan for 30 minutes. Flip bread out onto a piece of wax paper and flip it back over onto a serving platter, showing good side up.

For glaze mix powdered sugar and lemon juice on medium speed until dissolved. Sprinkle top of bread with almonds. Starting at one corner of bread, use a spoon and drizzle glaze in diagonal lines across bread.

"For you shall go out with joy, and be led out with peace;
The mountains and the hills shall break forth into singing before you,
And all the trees of the field will clap their hands."
Isaiah 55:12

Greek Sweet Bread

Ingredients:

1¼ cup warm water (105°-115°)
1 Tbsp. yeast
2 Tbsp. sugar

3 cups **GFM's Rice Coconut Blend Flour**
½ cup sugar
¾ tsp. salt
2 tsp. xanthan gum
1 tsp. orange zest, fresh or dried

1 egg
2 Tbsp. butter, melted
1 tsp. cider vinegar

1 egg, lightly beaten
1 Tbsp. milk

GFM Tip:
This bread will also taste great with **GFM's Rice Almond Blend Flour.**

Directions:

Spray 4x8 loaf pan with non-stick cooking spray.

In a liquid measuring cup stir together water, yeast and sugar until dissolved. Set aside 5 minutes until foamy.

In a stand mixer add flour, sugar, salt, xanthan gum and orange peel. Mix lightly to combine. Melt butter in microwave for 20 seconds. With mixer on low speed, pour yeast mixture into flour mixture. Then add egg, melted butter and vinegar. Turn mixer on high speed and beat for 2 minutes. Spread batter with rubber scraper evenly into prepared loaf pan, smoothing top. Let rise for 1 hour or until dough doubles in size.

Preheat oven to 400°. Whisk egg with milk and carefully spread over top of bread with pastry brush, being careful not to push bread down. Place bread on second lowest rack in oven. Bake for 30 minutes and then cover with foil without removing from oven and bake 30 minutes more, for a total baking time of 1 hour. Foil will prevent over browning.

"My son, give attention to my words; incline your ear to my sayings.
Do not let them depart from your eyes; keep them in the midst of your heart."
Proverbs 4:20-21

Herbed Onion Focaccia Bread

Ingredients:

1 cup warm water (105°-115°)
2¾ tsp. active dry yeast
1 Tbsp. sugar

3 cups **GFM's Rice Almond Blend Flour**
2 Tbsp. powdered milk
1½ tsp. xanthan gum
1 tsp. salt
1 tsp. rosemary
1 tsp. oregano
4 Tbsp. olive oil
1 egg + 1 egg white
1 tsp. cider vinegar
¼ onion, finely chopped

Herbed/Oil Topping:
⅓ cup olive oil
1 tsp. rosemary
1 tsp. oregano
1 clove garlic
2 Tbsp. onion

GFM Tip:
Sprinkle with cheddar cheese before baking for cheesy Focaccia bread.

"A merry heart does good like medicine;"
Proverbs 17:22

Directions:

Lightly spray 9 inch round or square cake pan with non-stick cooking spray. Stir warm water, yeast and sugar until dissolved. Set aside 5 minutes until foamy.

In a mixing bowl add flour, powdered milk, xanthan gum, salt, rosemary, oregano. Stir on low speed until combined. Slowly pour in yeast mixture. Add olive oil, egg and egg white, vinegar and onion. Stir on medium speed. Stop mixer and scrape down sides. Beat on high speed for 2 minutes. Dough should have appearance of a thick batter with a surface that can be smoothed with a rubber scraper. If dough is too dry add an extra tablespoon of oil or water. If too thin, add a tablespoon of flour. Spread dough into prepared pan. Let rise 1 hour or until double in size. Stir together oil, rosemary, oregano, garlic and onion for topping, set aside. Preheat oven to 400° about halfway through rising cycle.

After dough has risen, poke several holes with your finger tips across top of dough. Drizzle herb/oil mixture over dough, spreading evenly across top and into holes with a pastry brush or spoon. Bake in a preheated 400° oven on center rack for 25-30 minutes or until top is golden brown.

Variation for Pizza Crust: Prepare dough. Spray 2 small pizza pans with non-stick spray. Spread dough into two 8 inch rounds. Let rest 15 minutes. Bake in a preheated 400° oven for 10 minutes. Remove from oven, add your favorite pizza toppings, and bake for 20 minutes more or until cheese is melted and beginning to brown.

Honey Sandwich Bread

Ingredients: (Egg Free)

1 cup warm water (105°-115°)
1 Tbsp. sugar
1 Tbsp. yeast

3 cups **GFM's Rice Almond Blend Flour**
2 tsp. xanthan gum
¾ tsp. salt

2 Tbsp. melted butter
⅓ cup honey
⅓ cup applesauce, room temp.
1 tsp. cider vinegar

GFM Tip: Store honey at room temperature out of direct sunlight. If honey crystallizes, rejuvenate it to its liquid state by placing in a pan of hot water briefly.

Directions:

Spray a 4 x 8 inch bread pan with non-stick spray. In a liquid measuring cup combine warm water, sugar and yeast. Stir and set aside until foamy, about 5 minutes.

In a stand mixer bowl combine flour, xanthan gum and salt. Stir to combine. Melt butter in microwave 15-20 seconds. Measure out honey, applesauce and vinegar.

With mixer running on low speed, slowly pour yeast mixture into dry ingredients. With mixer continuing on low speed pour in butter, honey, applesauce, and vinegar. Stop mixer and scrape down sides of bowl. Beat on high speed for 3 minutes.

Spread dough evenly into prepared bread pan. Smooth out tops. Cover with towel and place in warm area to rise for 1-1½ hours or until doubled in size. Preheated oven to 375°. Place on second lowest rack in oven. Bake for 30 minutes and without removing from oven cover with foil and then continue baking for 30 minutes longer, for a total baking time of 1 hour. Foil prevents over browning.

Wait at least ½ hour before slicing bread for best results.

"My son, eat honey because it is good,
And the honeycomb which is sweet to your taste;
So shall be the knowledge of wisdom to your soul."
Proverbs 24:13,14

Mama's Monkey Bread

Ingredients:

⅓ cup warm water (105°-115°)
1 Tbsp. yeast
1 Tbsp. sugar

2¼ cups **GFM's Rice Almond Blend Flour**
1¼ tsp. xanthan gum
½ tsp. salt
¼ cup instant vanilla pudding mix
¼ cup sugar

½ cup + 1 Tbsp. buttermilk, room temp.
1 egg
½ tsp. cider vinegar

Coating:
1 tsp. cinnamon
¼ cup sugar

Topping:
¼ cup butter, melted
½ cup brown sugar
1 tsp. cinnamon

GFM Tip:
The trick in making this bread is keeping one hand lightly greased and the other hand dry. Work with your fingertips to roll in sugar and quickly move to pan.

"I sought the Lord and He heard me, and delivered me from all my fears."
Psalm 34:4

Directions:

Spray 9 x 5 inch bread pan with non-stick cooking spray and set aside. In a liquid measuring cup stir together water, yeast and sugar. Set aside 5 minutes until foamy.

In a stand mixer combine flour, xanthan gum, salt, vanilla pudding mix and sugar. Stir to combine. With mixer running on low slowly add yeast mixture, then buttermilk, egg, cider and vinegar. Stop mixer and scrape down sides of bowl. Beat on high speed for 3 minutes.

For coating combine sugar and cinnamon in a small bowl. Spray one hand (not your main hand) with non-stick cooking spray to prevent dough from sticking to your hand. Using a 1½ inch scoop, release rounded scoops of dough into greased hand. Use greased hand to roll dough ball in cinnamon sugar mixture to coat, then place in corner of prepared pan. Repeat until pan is full and all balls of dough are touching each other. Cover lightly with a towel and allow to rise in a warm place until doubled in size, about 1 hour and 15 minutes.

For topping melt butter in microwave safe bowl covered with waxed paper for 15 seconds. Stir brown sugar and cinnamon into the butter. Gently spread or pour cinnamon sugar mixture over entire surface of raised dough. Bake in preheated 375° oven just below center rack for 35-40 minutes, covering bread with foil after first 15 minutes of baking time to prevent brown sugar mixture from burning. Serve warm.

Mama's Zucchini Bread

Ingredients:

One Loaf

1¾ cups **GFM's Rice Almond Blend Flour**
¾ cup sugar
1 tsp. cinnamon
2 tsp. baking powder
¼ tsp. baking soda
¾ tsp. salt
1½ tsp. xanthan gum
½ cup chopped walnuts

2 eggs
1¼ cups grated zucchini
2 tsp. vanilla
¾ cup canola oil

GFM Tip:
Add 1 cup chocolate chips to make chocolate chip zucchini bread. Kids will love it!

Directions:

Preheat oven to 350°. Spray a 4x8 inch bread pan with non-stick cooking spray.

In a medium bowl add flour, sugar, cinnamon, baking powder, soda, salt, xanthan gum and walnuts. Whisk to combine and set aside.

In stand mixer bowl combine eggs, zucchini, vanilla and oil. Beat for 1 minute on medium speed.

Add half of flour mixture to wet ingredients and mix slowly just until slightly combined. Add remaining flour and repeat. Do not over mix. If batter appears too wet and will not form peaks, add 1-2 tablespoons extra GF flour.

Spread batter into prepared bread pan. Lightly sprinkle top of bread with sugar. Place bread just below the second lowest rack in oven. Bake in preheated 350° oven for 1 hour, covering bread with foil without removing from oven, the last 15 minutes of baking time. Knife inserted into center should come out clean. Allow to cool for ½ hour before slicing.

"Hope deferred makes the heart sick, but when the desire comes, it is a tree of life."
Proverbs 13:12

Mama's Two Loaf Zucchini Bread

Ingredients:

Two Loaves

3½ cups **GFM's Rice Almond Blend Flour**
1½ cups sugar
2 tsp. cinnamon
2 tsp. baking powder
½ tsp. baking soda
1½ tsp. salt
2 tsp. xanthan gum
1 cup chopped walnuts

4 eggs
2½ cups grated zucchini
2 tsp. vanilla
1½ cups canola oil

GFM Tip:
Eat one loaf and freeze one for later!

Directions:

Preheat oven to 350°. Spray two 4x8 inch bread pans with non-stick cooking spray.

In a medium bowl add flour, sugar, cinnamon, baking powder, soda, salt, xanthan gum and walnuts. Whisk to combine and set aside.

In stand mixer bowl combine eggs, zucchini, vanilla and oil. Beat for 1 minute on medium speed.

Add half of flour mixture to wet ingredients and mix slowly just until slightly combined. Add remaining flour and repeat. Do not over mix. If batter appears too wet and will not form peaks, add 1-2 tablespoons extra GF flour.

Spread half of the batter into each bread pan. Lightly sprinkle tops of bread with sugar. Place bread on second lowest rack. Bake in preheated 350° oven for 1 hour, covering bread with foil without removing from oven, the last 15 minutes of baking time. Knife inserted into center should come out clean. Allow to cool for 30 minutes before slicing.

"But let him ask in faith, with no doubting,
for he who doubts is like a wave of the sea driven and tossed by the wind."
James 1:6

Oatmeal Bread

Ingredients:

¾ cup warm water (105°-115°)
1 scant Tbsp. yeast
1 Tbsp. sugar

3 cups **GFM's Rice Almond Blend Flour**
1½ tsp. xanthan gum
¾ tsp. salt
1½ tsp. cinnamon
1 cup toasted oatmeal * (certified GF oats)

¾ cup buttermilk, room temperature
3 Tbsp. honey
2 Tbsp. butter, melted
1 egg white
1 tsp. cider vinegar

1-2 Tbsp. certified GF oats

GFM Tip:
To toast oatmeal spread evenly onto a baking sheet. Bake in 300° oven for 5-10 minutes or until golden brown. Watch closely to prevent from burning.

Directions:

Spray 4x8 inch loaf bread pan with non-stick coating.

In a large measuring cup, stir together warm water, yeast and sugar. Set aside 5 minutes until foamy.

In a stand mixer add flour, xanthan gum, salt, cinnamon and toasted oatmeal. Stir until combined.

With mixer running on low speed, slowly add yeast mixture. Stop the mixer and add the buttermilk, honey, butter, egg white and cider vinegar. Mix on low speed until combined. Scrape down sides of bowl. Beat on high speed for 2-3 minutes. Spread evenly into prepared bread pan. Sprinkle lightly with untoasted GF oats. Cover with light weight towel and let rise one hour or until doubled in size.

Preheat oven to 400°. Place bread on second lowest rack in oven. Bake for 30 minutes and then without removing from oven gently cover with foil and continue to bake for 30 minutes longer, for a total baking time of 1 hour. Foil prevents over browning. Cool for 30 minutes before slicing.

Note: If using a glass bread pan, reduce oven temperature to 375°.

"The word of the Lord is proven;
He is a shield to all who trust Him."
Psalm 18:30

Old Fashioned Potato Bread

Ingredients:

⅔ cup potato, peeled and chopped
½ cup potato water

½ cup warm water (105°-115°)
1 scant Tbsp. yeast
1 Tbsp. sugar

3 cups **GFM's Rice Almond Blend Flour**
1½ tsp. xanthan gum
¾ tsp. salt

2 Tbsp. butter, melted
½ cup buttermilk
1 egg
1 tsp. cider vinegar

GFM Tip:
If using glass bread pan, reduce oven temperature to 375°.

Directions:

Spray 4x8 bread pan with non-stick oil spray. Fill a sauce pan with 1 inch of water and add chopped potato. Boil for about 6-8 minutes or until potato is tender. Reserve ½ cup of potato water and drain off rest of water. Pour reserved water back into pan and mash potato chunks into water.

While potatoes are cooking, stir together warm water, yeast and sugar. Set aside 5 minutes until foamy.

In a stand mixer add flour, xanthan gum, and salt. Mix lightly to combine.

Melt butter in microwave safe dish covered with waxed paper for about 15 seconds. In a small bowl, whisk together buttermilk, egg and vinegar.

Add buttermilk mixture and butter to mashed potato. Mix well. With mixer on low speed, add yeast mixture, then slowly add potato/buttermilk mixture. Beat on high speed 2-3 minutes. Spread evenly into bread pan. Cover and let rise for 1 hour or until doubled.

Preheat oven to 400°. Place bread on second lowest rack in oven. Bake bread for 30 minutes and then without removing from oven gently cover with foil and bake and additional 30 minutes, for a total baking time of 1 hour. Foil prevents over browning. Allow to cool for 30 minutes before slicing.

"The Lord bless you and keep you; the LORD make his face shine upon you, and be gracious to you: The LORD lift up His countenance upon you and give you peace."
Numbers 6:24-26

Rosemary Potato Bread

Ingredients:

⅔ cup potato, peeled and chopped
½ cup potato water

½ warm water (105°-115°)
1 scant Tbsp. yeast
1 Tbsp. sugar

3 cups **GFM's Rice Almond Blend Flour**
1½ tsp. xanthan gum
¾ tsp. salt
1 Tbsp. dried rosemary needles, crushed
2 tsp. dried parsley

2 Tbsp. margarine, melted
½ cup buttermilk
1 egg
1 tsp. cider vinegar

GFM Tip:
Freeze leftover herbs. Wash and dry them and place in freezer bags with the date. Herbs can safely be frozen for up to three months.

"Give us this day our daily bread.
And forgive us our debts,
as we forgive our debtors"
Matthew 6:11

Directions:

Spray 4x8 bread pan with non-stick oil spray. Fill a sauce pan with 1 inch of water and add chopped potato. Boil for about 6-8 minutes or until potato is tender. Reserve ½ cup of potato water and drain off rest of water. Pour reserved water back into pan and mash potato chunks into water.

Stir together warm water, yeast and sugar until dissolved. Set aside 5 minutes until foamy.

In a stand mixer add flour, xanthan gum and salt. Crush rosemary needles in a mortar and pestle until flavor is released and texture is fine but not powdery. Crush parsley lightly with fingers to release flavor. Add herbs to flour mixture and mix lightly to combine. Melt margarine in microwave safe dish covered with waxed paper for 15 seconds. In a small bowl, whisk together buttermilk, egg and vinegar.

Add buttermilk mixture and margarine to mashed potatoes. Mix well. With mixer on low speed, add yeast mixture, then slowly add potato/buttermilk mixture to dry ingredients. Beat on high speed for 3 minutes. Spread evenly into prepared bread pan. Smooth top with a buttered spatula. Cover with a light weight towel and let rise for 1 hour or until double in size.

Preheat oven to 400°. Place bread on second lowest rack in oven. Bake for 30 minutes and then without removing from oven cover with foil and then bake for 30 minutes longer, for a total baking time of 1 hour. Remove bread from pan to cooling rack and allow to cool 20 minutes before slicing.

Biscuits, Rolls and Buns

"Most assuredly, I say to you, Moses did not give you the bread from heaven, but My Father gives you the true bread from heaven. For the bread of God is He who comes down from heaven and gives life to the world."
John 6:32-33

Cheese and Onion Drop Biscuits

Ingredients:

2 cups **GFM's Rice Almond Blend Flour**
2 tsp. baking powder
1 tsp. xanthan gum
½ tsp. salt
¼ tsp. garlic powder

1 cup buttermilk
½ cup butter
2 Tbsp. water
1 egg
1 Tbsp. honey
¼ cup fresh green onion, minced
2 Tbsp. fresh or dried parsley
1 cup shredded cheddar cheese,
or pizza blend,

GFM Tip: Make them breadsticks by forming into long 4-5 inch long sticks. Sprinkle tops with more cheese if desired. Serve with Marinara sauce.

Directions:

Preheat oven to 450°. In a medium bowl combine flour, baking powder, xanthan gum, salt and garlic powder. Whisk lightly with a fork until combined.

In a glass bowl measure out buttermilk and add stick of butter to buttermilk. Heat buttermilk and butter in microwave for 45 seconds or until butter is soft. Butter does not have to be completely melted, just pliable with a spoon. Pour buttermilk mixture into a mixing bowl. Add water, egg, honey, green onion, parsley and cheese to buttermilk mixture. Mix on medium speed until well combined. Add half of flour mixture and mix on low speed for 10 seconds. Repeat with remaining flour.

Remove mixing bowl from mixer and continue mixing dough by folding batter until flour is completely mixed into wet ingredients. Drop by large spoonfuls onto a greased cookie sheet. Smooth out tops with finger or greased spoon. Bake in preheated 450° oven for 12-14 minutes or until tops and bottoms are a light golden brown. Serve warm.

"My grace is sufficient for you, for My strength is made perfect in weakness."
2 Corinthians 12:9

Cheesy Drop Biscuits for Two

Ingredients:

1⅛ cups **GFM's Rice Almond Blend Flour**
1½ tsp. baking powder
¼ tsp. salt
½ tsp. xanthan gum
1 Tbsp. parsley
¼ tsp. garlic powder

¼ cup butter, melted
1 egg
½ cup milk
1 Tbsp. honey
2 Tbsp. green onion, minced
½ cup cheddar cheese, shredded

GFM Tip:
Try using fresh minced garlic in place of garlic powder.

Directions:

Preheat oven to 450°. Lightly spray cookie sheet with non-stick spray. In a medium bowl combine flour, baking powder, salt, xanthan gum, parsley and garlic powder. Whisk lightly with a fork and set aside.

In a medium bowl add melted butter, egg, milk, honey and green onion. Mix well by hand. Stir in cheddar cheese until combined. Add flour mixture all at once to wet ingredients and mix by hand with a wooden spoon just until combined. Do not over mix.

Drop dough by ¼ cup measure onto lightly greased cookie sheet. Bake in preheated 450° oven for 10-12 minutes, or until tops are light golden brown. Serve Warm.

Yield: 6 Biscuits.

"Now faith is the substance of things hoped for, the evidence of things not seen."
Hebrews 11:1

Cinnamon Rolls

Ingredients:

⅓ cup warm water
2½ tsp. yeast
1 Tbsp. sugar

1¾ cups **GFM's Rice Almond Blend Flour**
1¼ tsp. xanthan gum
½ tsp. salt
3 Tbsp. instant vanilla pudding mix

½ cup milk
1 egg
½ tsp. cider vinegar

Filling:
¼ cup butter
½ cup brown sugar
1 tsp. cinnamon

GFM Tip:
Warm cinnamon rolls in microwave 10-15 seconds to rejuvenate.

"Watch, stand fast in the faith, be brave, be strong."
1 Corinthians: 16:13

Directions:

Grease 8 muffin cups on a muffin pan. Set aside. In a liquid measuring cup dissolve water, yeast and sugar. Set aside 5 minutes until foamy.

In a stand mixer add flour, xanthan gum, salt and vanilla pudding mix. Mix on low speed until combined. With mixer on low speed slowly pour in yeast mixture, then milk, egg and cider vinegar. Stop mixer and scrape down sides of bowl. Beat 2 minutes on high speed.

For filling, partially melt butter in microwave 10 seconds. Stir in brown sugar and cinnamon. Mix well. Using a small cookie scoop, place 1 inch rounds of batter into bottoms of eight greased muffin cups. Spread evenly with spoon making ¼ to ½ inch thickness at bottoms of muffin cups. Spoon rounded teaspoon portions of filling onto top of batter in each muffin cup. Repeat by adding alternating layers of batter and filling until the batter reaches top of muffin cup. Be sure to gently spread batter evenly over top of filling. With a knife make a swirl motion throughout tops of cinnamon roll. Cover and let rise for 45 minutes.

Preheat oven to 350°. Bake for 20 minutes or until tops are light golden brown.

Let cinnamon rolls cool in muffin tin 10 minutes before removing. Gently remove each cinnamon roll from pan by flipping pan over onto a clean surface, or by gently loosening with a table knife. Frost with Cream Cheese Icing. Serve Warm.

***Refer to Frostings and Icing section for Cream Cheese Icing recipe.**

Easy Italian Dinner Rolls

Ingredients:

1½ cups **GFM's Rice Almond Blend Flour**
1 tsp. xanthan gum
½ tsp. salt
2 tsp. baking powder
½ tsp. Italian seasoning
½ tsp. garlic powder

½ cup buttermilk, or milk
2 eggs, lightly beaten
¼ cup butter, melted
¼ cup onion, minced
2 Tbsp. honey
½ tsp. cider vinegar (optional)

Directions:

Preheat oven to 400°. Spray 6 muffin cups with non-stick cooking spray.

In a medium bowl combine flour, xanthan gum, salt, baking powder, Italian seasoning and garlic powder. Mix lightly with a fork to combine. Set aside.

In a small bowl combine buttermilk or milk, eggs, butter, onion, honey and vinegar. Whisk lightly for about 20 seconds until well combined. Pour wet ingredients onto dry ingredients and mix with a large spoon just until combined.

Scoop dough evenly into 6 greased muffin cups. Smooth out tops of rolls with spoon for good presentation. Bake in preheated 400° oven just above center rack for 12-14 minutes or until tops are golden brown. Serve warm.

Variation: Spoon dough into 6 evenly formed mounds. Smooth tops with rubber scraper. Bake 12-14 minutes or until tops are golden brown.

GFM Tip: Make it Pizza! Prepare as directed. Flatten into two 6 inch rounds. Bake in preheated oven for 5-8 minutes. Remove from oven add pizza sauce, cheese and desired toppings. Bake 10-12 minutes or until cheese is melted.

"Give thanks to the Lord, for He is good, His mercy endures forever."
Psalm 106:1

Perfect Hamburger Buns

Ingredients:

1 cup warm water (105°-115°)
1 Tbsp. yeast
1 Tbsp. sugar

3 cups **GFM's Rice Almond Blend Flour**
1½ tsp. xanthan gum
¼ cup powdered instant milk
(or dairy free alternative)
¾ tsp. salt

1 egg
¼ cup honey
¼ cup butter or margarine, melted
1 tsp. cider vinegar

(optional)
*egg white and 1 Tbsp. milk
*sesame seeds
*minced onion (for dried minced onion, soak in 3 Tbsp. of water for 5 min.)

GFM Tip: You don't need a hamburger bun pan to make beautiful hamburger buns, but it is nice to have for the perfect shape and size. You can also use 4 inch cake pans made by Wilton to form a nice bun. Whatever you decide, don't let not having the perfect pan prevent you from enjoying this incredible gluten free hamburger bun!

Directions:

Prepare baking pan by spraying with non-stick spray. In a liquid measuring cup mix together warm water, yeast and sugar. Set aside for about 5 minutes until foamy.

In a stand mixer bowl combine flour, xanthan gum, instant milk and salt. Mix on low speed until combined. Break egg in bowl and measure out honey. Melt butter in microwave safe bowl covered with waxed paper for 15 seconds. Measure vinegar and add to butter.

With mixer running on low speed, slowly pour yeast mixture into dry ingredients. Pour in honey, butter and egg. Stop mixer and scrape down sides of bowl. Beat on high speed for 3 minutes. Beating 3 minutes will allow buns to develop a texture similar to regular hamburger buns.

Scoop ⅓ cup dough onto cookie sheet or bun pan, forming a 4 inch circle. Smooth out tops. Gently cover with a light weight towel and allow to rise in a warm place for 1½ hours, or until doubled.

For a shiny crust, lightly brush egg white mixed with 1 tablespoon milk over tops of buns. Sprinkle with sesame seeds or onions. Bake in preheated 375° oven just above center rack for 15-18 minutes or until tops are golden brown.

Yield: 6-8 buns.

"And be kind to one another, tenderhearted, forgiving one another, even as God in Christ forgave you."
Ephesians 4:32

Southern Buttermilk Biscuits

Ingredients:

2 cups **GFM's Rice Almond Blend Flour**
2 tsp. baking powder
1 tsp. baking soda
½ tsp. salt
1 tsp. xanthan gum

¼ cup butter, softened
¾ cup buttermilk
3 Tbsp. honey
1 egg, lightly beaten

GFM Tip:
These biscuits are great for biscuits and gravy or served with honey butter.

Directions:

Lightly spray baking sheet with non-stick cooking spray. Preheat oven to 425°.

In a medium bowl combine flour, baking powder, soda, salt and xanthan gum. Whisk lightly with a fork to combine. Make a well in center of flour mixture. Soften butter 20 seconds in small microwave bowl covered with waxed paper. Pour butter, buttermilk, honey and lightly beaten egg into dry ingredients. With a wooden spoon or spatula stir mixture by hand until combined. Dough will be slightly thick and sticky.

Drop dough by ¼ cup measure onto prepared cookie sheet and gently press tops with palm of hand until ½ - ¾ inch thick. Gently press in sides to form a circle to resemble a rolled, cut out biscuit, but without all the work. Use back of spoon to smooth tops if need.

Bake 2 inches apart in preheated 425° oven for 12-15 minutes, or until tops are golden brown. Serve warm.

Yield: 8-10 very tasty biscuits!

*"This is the day which the LORD has made;
we will rejoice and be glad in it."
Psalm 118:24*

Muffins and Scones

"The word of God is living and powerful, and sharper than any two-edged sword, piercing even to the division of soul and spirit, and of joints and marrow, and is a discerner of the thoughts and intents of the heart."
Hebrews 4:12

Apple Cinnamon Muffins

Ingredients:

1¾ cups **GFM's Rice Almond Blend Flour**
1½ tsp. xanthan gum
2 tsp. baking powder
½ tsp. salt
¼ tsp. allspice
1 tsp. cinnamon

½ cup milk
¼ cup oil
½ cup applesauce
2 eggs
½ cup sugar

1 apple, chopped

GFM Tip: Coat apple pieces with 1 tablespoon of the flour to keep them from sinking to the bottom of the muffin.

Directions:

Preheat oven to 400°. Line muffin pan with 12 muffin liners.

In a medium bowl combine flour, xanthan gum, baking powder, salt, allspice and cinnamon. Whisk to combine and set aside.

In a stand mixer combine milk, oil, applesauce, eggs and sugar. Mix on high speed for 1 minute. Add flour mixture to wet ingredients and mix on low speed just until combined. Fold in chopped apple pieces.

Spoon batter into prepared muffin pan filling each muffin liners nearly full. Bake in 400° preheated oven for 20 minutes or until golden brown.

Yield: 12 delicious muffins

"The grass withers, and the flower fades,
But the Word of our God stands forever."
Isaiah 40:8

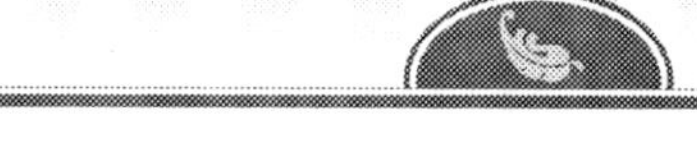

Blueberry Yogurt Muffins

Ingredients:

2 cups **GFM's Rice Almond Blend Flour**
2 tsp. baking powder
1¼ tsp. xanthan gum
¼ tsp. salt

½ cup butter, room temperature
1 cup sugar
1 8 oz. carton GF vanilla yogurt
1 egg
1 tsp. vanilla
¼ cup heavy cream, or milk
2 cups frozen blueberries

2 Tbsp. sugar, for sprinkling

GFM Tip: Allowing blueberries to begin to thaw will make batter more pliable. The partially frozen blueberries will cause dough to become very thick. This thickness does not affect taste or presentation of finished product.

Directions:

Preheat oven to 375°. Line muffin tins with muffin liners. Measure out blueberries and set aside to begin to thaw while making batter.

In a medium bowl combine flour, baking powder, xanthan gum and salt. Lightly whisk flour mixture with a fork until combined. Set aside.

In a stand mixer cream butter until light and fluffy. Add sugar, yogurt, egg, vanilla and cream or milk. Beat 1 minute on medium speed until well combined. Stop mixer and add half of flour mixture. Mix on lowest speed for 10 seconds or just long enough to combine the flour. Repeat with remaining flour. Remove mixing bowl from mixer and finish lightly folding batter just until flour is mixed into wet ingredients. Be careful not to over mix batter. Fold in blueberries distributing evenly throughout batter. Fill muffin liners to top with muffin batter. Smooth out tops with finger or greased spoon. Lightly sprinkle tops of muffins with sugar.

Bake in preheated 375° oven on center rack for 25-30 minutes or until tops are light golden brown and toothpick inserted in center comes out clean.

"With men it is impossible, but not with God; for with God all things are possible."
Mark 10:27

Buttermilk Apple Muffins

Ingredients:

1¾ cups **GFM's Rice Almond Blend Flour**
2 tsp. baking powder
1 tsp. xanthan gum
¾ tsp. salt
1½ tsp. cinnamon

1 egg
¾ cup buttermilk
⅓ cup canola oil
¼ cup brown sugar, packed
½ cup sugar
½ cup applesauce
1 tsp. vanilla
1 cup apples, chopped small
⅓ cup walnuts or raisins (optional)

2 Tbsp. sugar (for sprinkling)

GFM Tip: When using baking powder be sure not to over beat your mix. Mix dry ingredients into the wet ingredients just until blended for best results.

Directions:

Preheat oven to 350°. Line muffin tin with 12 baking liners. In a medium bowl combine flour, baking powder, xanthan gum, salt and cinnamon. Mix lightly, set aside.

In a separate mixing bowl beat together egg and buttermilk for about 30 seconds by hand. Add oil, brown sugar, sugar, applesauce, vanilla and apples pieces. Mix together well. Pour dry ingredients into wet ingredients. With a wooden spoon mix just until all ingredients are combined. Fold in walnuts or raisins if desired.

Fill muffin cups nearly to rim. Lightly sprinkle tops of muffins with sugar. Place in preheated 350°oven for 28-30 minutes or until tops are lightly browned and toothpick inserted in middle comes out clean. Let cool completely before serving.

"So then Faith comes by hearing, and hearing by the Word of God."
Romans 10:17

Chocolate Orange Muffins

Ingredients:

2 cups **GFM's Rice Almond Blend Flour**
1¼ tsp. xanthan gum
½ tsp. baking soda
1½ tsp. baking powder
½ tsp. salt

½ cup hot water
½ cup unsweetened cocoa powder
2 Tbsp. orange juice concentrate
2 tsp. vanilla

½ cup margarine
1¼ cups sugar
2 large eggs

Glaze:
½ cup powdered sugar
1 Tbsp. orange juice concentrate

GFM Tip:
For warm muffins the next day, place in microwave for 15-20 seconds.

Directions:

Preheat oven to 350°. Line muffin cups with paper liners.

In a medium bowl add flour xanthan gum, baking soda, baking powder and salt. Whisk to combine and set aside.

Add cocoa to hot water and whisk to dissolve. Add orange juice concentrate and vanilla to cocoa mixture. Set aside.

With a stand mixer, beat margarine and sugar 3-4 minutes until sugar is dissolved and mixture is light and fluffy. Add eggs one at a time, beating well after each. Add cocoa mixture and beat well. Add flour mixture to wet mixture all at once and mix by hand just until flour is completely dispersed. Do not over mix batter. Let batter rest 20 minutes to allow for the best raised muffin.

Do not disturb batter by mixing, but carefully scoop out and fill muffin cups nearly full. Bake for 20 minutes in preheated 350° oven. Remove from oven and let cool in muffin pan 3 minutes before removing each muffin to cooling rack.

Mix powdered sugar and orange juice together. Drizzle glaze over warm muffins.

"For You are my hope, O Lord God; you are my trust from my youth."
Psalm 71:5

Cranberry Scones

Ingredients: (egg free)

1¼ cups **GFM's Rice Almond Blend Flour**
⅓ cup sugar
2 tsp. baking powder
½ tsp. xanthan gum
½ tsp. salt
2 tsp. orange zest, fresh or dried

¾ cup heavy cream (whipping cream)
½ cup Craisins (dried cranberries)

2-3 Tbsp. heavy cream (for basting)
2 Tbsp. sugar (for sprinkling)

GFM Tip:
Serve warm with a hot glass of you favorite herbal tea!

Directions:

Preheat oven to 375°

Mix flour, sugar, baking powder, xanthan gum, salt and orange zest in a stand mixing bowl until well combined. Add cream and mix on lowest speed just until combined. Fold in Craisins with hands.

Remove dough from mixing bowl press dough with hands from center out into round 8 inch circle shape directly on an ungreased cookie sheet. The dough should be a half inch or more thick.

After dough is shaped into circle, cut into 6-8 wedges and separate slightly. Baste with cream, and sprinkle lightly with sugar.

Bake in preheated 375° oven just above center rack for 20-22 minutes or until tops are a golden brown.

"I desire therefore that the men pray everywhere,
lifting up holy hands, without wrath and doubting."
1 Timothy 2:8

Ginger Peach Muffins

Ingredients:

2 cups **GFM's Rice Almond Blend Flour**
1¼ tsp. xanthan gum
2 tsp. baking powder
½ tsp. salt
½ tsp. ground ginger
⅛ tsp. ground cloves
½ cup crystallized ginger, packed small pieces

½ cup butter
1 cup sugar
2 tsp. vanilla
2 Tbsp. peach juice concentrate
or white grape peach juice, optional
1 egg
1 cup heavy cream

¾-1 cup diced peaches, fresh
2 Tbsp. Sugar, for sprinkling

GFM Tip:
You can buy crystallized ginger in the Asian isle at the grocery store or at most health food stores. It is very affordable and offers a great flavor.

Directions:

Preheat oven to 350°. Line muffin pan with muffin liners. In a large bowl combine flour, xanthan gum, baking powder, salt, ground ginger, cloves, and ginger pieces. Mix lightly with a fork until combined.

In a stand mixer bowl cream butter, sugar and vanilla until light and fluffy. Add peach juice and egg and mix for 30 seconds. With mixer on low speed, alternate adding flour and cream until both are completely mixed in. Remove bowl from mixer and fold in peach pieces by hand, distributing evenly throughout batter.

Using a ¼ cup measure, scoop batter into muffin cup liners filling 12 muffin cups equally to the rim of liner. Sprinkle tops lightly with sugar. Bake in preheated 350° oven 25-30 minutes. Top of muffins should be lightly browned and toothpick inserted in center should come out clean. Allow muffins to remain in pan for 10 minutes before transferring to cooling rack.

Yield: 12 muffins

*Note: Using a 1½ inch cookie scoop works great for filling muffin cups evenly.

"If we confess our sins, He is faithful and just to forgive us our sins and to cleanse us from all unrighteousness."
1 John 1:9

Mandarin Chocolate Chip Muffins

Ingredients:

2 cups **GFM's Rice Almond Blend Flour**
2 tsp. baking powder
1¼ tsp. xanthan gum
¼ tsp. salt
1 tsp. orange zest

½ cup butter or margarine, room temp.
1 cup sugar
1 egg
1 tsp. vanilla
½ cup heavy cream or milk
1 11oz. can of mandarin oranges
¼ cup liquid from mandarin oranges
1 cup mini chocolate chips

1 cup coconut flakes

GFM Tip:
This recipe will also work well with **GFM's Rice Coconut Blend Flour.**

Directions:

Preheat oven to 350°. Line muffin tins with muffin cup liners. In a medium bowl combine flour, baking powder, xanthan gum, salt and orange zest. Lightly whisk flour mixture with a fork until combined and set aside.

In a stand mixer beat butter until light and fluffy. Drain mandarin oranges, reserving ¼ cup of juice. Add sugar, egg, vanilla, cream, and reserved mandarin orange juice. Beat on medium speed for 30-60 seconds. With mixer running on slow speed add flour mixture slowly. Add chocolate chips and stir on low until combined. Remove bowl from mixer. Gently fold mandarin oranges into the batter, being careful not to break them up.

Scoop batter into muffin liner, filling each cup to rim of liner. Sprinkle tops with coconut flakes. Bake in preheated 350° oven on center rack for 25-30 minutes, or until tops are golden brown and toothpick inserted in center comes out clean. Allow muffins to remain in muffin pan for 10 minutes before transferring to a cooling rack.

Yield: 12 muffins.

"The thief does not come except to steal, and to kill, and to destroy.
I have come that they might have life, and that they might have it more abundantly."
John 10:10

Oatmeal Apple Crisp Muffins

Ingredients:

2 cups **GFM's Rice Almond Blend Flour**
¼ tsp. salt
1½ tsp. xanthan gum
1 tsp. cinnamon
2 tsp. baking powder

½ cup butter or margarine, room temp.
½ cup brown sugar, packed
½ cup sugar
2 tsp. vanilla
1 egg
1 cup heavy cream
¾ cup Certified GF Oats
1 cup apple pieces, diced

Topping:

3 Tbsp. butter or margarine
2 Tbsp. brown sugar
2 Tbsp. Certified GF Oats
1 Tbsp. **GFM's Rice Almond Blend Flour**
1 tsp. cinnamon

GFM Tip:
Save time by creaming the butter and sugar while you are preparing the dry ingredients.

Directions:

Preheat oven to 375°. Line muffin pan with muffin cup liners. In a medium bowl combine flour, salt, xanthan gum, cinnamon and baking powder. Mix lightly with a fork to combine. Set aside.

In a stand mixer, cream butter, brown sugar, and sugar 1-2 minutes until light and fluffy. Add vanilla, and egg. Beat for 1 minute on medium speed. Add cream, oats, and apple pieces. Mix on medium speed until well combined. Stop mixer and add half of flour mixture. Mix on low speed just until combined. Add remaining flour and repeat. Remove bowl from mixer and gently fold batter with rubber scraper until all flour is combined into wet mixture.

Scoop batter into prepared muffin liners. Fill each muffin cup with batter to rim of muffin liner.

In a glass bowl, combine butter and sugar. Heat in microwave for 15 seconds, or until melted. Stir oats, flour and cinnamon into the butter mixture. Spread a small spoonful of mixture across top of each muffin.

Bake in preheated 375° oven 25-28 minutes or until tops are golden brown and bounce back when touched. A toothpick inserted in the center should come out clean.

Yield: 12 muffins.

"...Eye has not seen, nor ear heard, nor have entered into the heart of man, the things which God has prepared for those who love him."
1 Corinthians 2:9

Raspberry Yogurt Swirl Muffins

Ingredients:

2 cups **GFM's Rice Almond Blend Flour**
2 tsp. baking powder
1¼ tsp. xanthan gum
¼ tsp. salt

½ cup butter or margarine, room temp.
1 cup sugar
1 8oz. carton GF vanilla yogurt
2 Tbsp. frozen raspberry juice concentrate
1 egg
1 tsp. vanilla
2 cups frozen raspberries
2 Tbsp. sugar

GFM Tip:
If you don't have frozen juice concentrate replace with heavy cream or milk.

Directions:

Preheat oven to 375°. Line muffin tins with muffin cup liners. In a medium bowl combine flour, baking powder, xanthan gum, and salt. Lightly whisk flour mixture with a fork until combined and set aside.

In a stand mixer beat butter and sugar until light and fluffy. Add yogurt, raspberry concentrate, egg and vanilla. Beat for 1 minute on medium speed until well combined. Stop the mixer and add half of flour mixture. Mix on low speed for 10 seconds or just long enough to combine flour. Repeat with remaining flour. Remove mixing bowl from mixer and finish folding flour into batter just until flour is well mixed. Do not over mix batter. Fold in raspberries. The raspberries will naturally make a swirl through the batter for a beautiful presentation. Again, do not over mix.

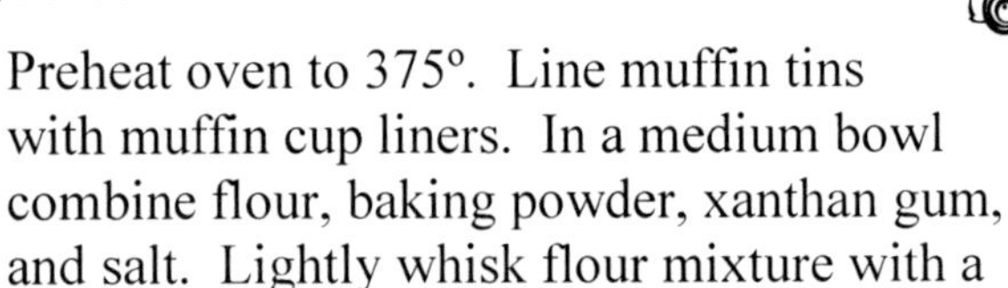

Fill muffin cup liners to rim with muffin batter. Smooth tops with finger or greased spoon. Lightly sprinkle tops of muffins with sugar. Bake in preheated 375° oven on center rack for 25-30 minutes or until tops are light golden brown and toothpick inserted in center comes out clean.

Yield: 1 dozen muffins

"Do not be conformed to this world, but be transformed by the renewing of your mind that you may prove what is that good and acceptable and perfect will of God."
Romans 12:2

Scrumptious Cranberry Orange Scones

Ingredients:

1⅔ cups **GFM's Rice Almond Blend Flour**
⅓ cup sugar
½ cup powdered sugar
½ tsp. salt
2 tsp. fresh grated orange peel
1 tsp. xanthan gum
3 tsp. baking powder

4 Tbsp. butter, melted
1 egg + 1 egg white
½ cup buttermilk
2 rounded Tbsp. orange juice concentrate

½ cup dried cranberries
2 Tbsp. sugar, for sprinkling

GFM Tip: Use fresh cranberries when in season. Coat them with ¼ cup sugar.

Directions:

Preheat oven to 350°. In a large bowl add flour, sugar, powdered sugar, salt, orange peel, xanthan gum and baking powder. Whisk lightly until combined.

In a separate bowl add butter, eggs, buttermilk and orange juice concentrate. Beat with wire whisk until well combined. Add liquid ingredients to dry ingredients bowl. Mix lightly, just until combined. Gently fold in cranberries.

Option 1: Drop by ¼ cup measure onto a cookie sheet. Smooth out tops and lightly sprinkle with sugar. Bake in a preheated 350° oven 18-20 minutes. When done, scones should be lightly brown and springy when touched.

Option 2: Lightly grease and coat an 8 inch round cake pan with GF flour. Lightly sprinkle with sugar. Spread batter about ¾ inch thick into pan. Bake in preheated 350° oven for 22-25 minutes until top is slightly brown and knife inserted in center comes out clean.

"Bless the LORD, O my soul, ...Who redeems your life from destruction;
Who crowns you with loving kindness and tender mercies;"
Psalm 103:2,4

White Chocolate Raspberry Scones

Ingredients:

1¾ cups **GFM's Rice Almond Blend Flour**
2 tsp. baking powder
¼ tsp. salt
¾ tsp xanthan gum

6 Tbsp. butter
¾ cup sugar
1 tsp. vanilla
1 egg

½ cup white chocolate chips, melted
¾ cup heavy cream
1¼ cups frozen raspberries

2 Tbsp. heavy cream (for basting)
1 Tbsp. sugar (for dusting)

GFM Tip:
Don't take raspberries out of the freezer until ready to use. It helps prevent them from breaking apart when folding in.

Directions:

Preheat oven to 375°. In a medium bowl combine flour, baking powder, salt and xanthan gum. Whisk lightly with a fork to combine and set aside.

In a stand mixer cream butter, sugar and vanilla until light and fluffy. Scrape down sides of bowl. Add egg and beat well on medium speed for about 30 seconds.

Melt chocolate chips in microwave at 70% power for about 1 minute until melted. Fold melted white chocolate into the butter mixture.

With mixer running on low speed, alternately add small portions of flour and heavy cream until both are combined. Remove mixing bowl from mixer. Scrape down sides of bowl.

Fold in raspberries, taking care not to break them up to much.

Place about ¼ cup rounded scoops of batter onto a lightly greased cookie sheet 2 inches apart. Smooth out tops with fingers. Using a basting brush, lightly baste with heavy cream. Sprinkle tops with sugar.

Place in preheated 375° oven just above center rack for 18-20 minutes or until tops just begin to brown. Remove from oven and allow to remain on cookie sheet 1 minute before transferring to a cooling rack.

Serve warm.

"The fruit of the Spirit is love, joy, peace, longsuffering, kindness, goodness, faithfulness, gentleness, self-control."
Galatians 5:22-23

Cakes and Brownies

"Oh, taste and see that the LORD is good;
Blessed is the man who trusts in Him!"
Psalm 34:8

Almond Pound Cake

Ingredients:

2 cups **GFM's Rice Almond Blend Flour**
2 tsp. baking powder
1 tsp. lemon zest
¼ tsp. salt
1¼ tsp. xanthan gum

¾ cup + 2 Tbsp. butter, softened
1 cup sugar
1 tsp. almond extract
2 tsp. vanilla extract
5 eggs

GFM Tip: This pound cake is meant to be served in wedges like a pie vs. traditional bread style slices. If you prefer a traditional style, bake in a loaf pan 15 minutes longer or until top bounces back when touched.

Directions:

Preheat oven to 350°. Grease and lightly dust a 9 inch round cake pan with GF flour.

In a medium bowl combine flour, baking powder, lemon zest, salt and xanthan gum. Whisk lightly with a fork and set aside.

In a stand mixer cream butter, sugar, vanilla and almond extract until light and fluffy. With mixer on low speed add eggs one at a time. Add half of flour mixture to wet ingredients and mix on low speed 10 seconds. Repeat with remaining flour. Stop mixer and scrape down sides. Mix on low speed 30 seconds more, or until flour is completely mixed in.

Pour batter into prepared cake pan. Smooth top evenly with rubber scraper. Gently tap and shake sides of pan to even out batter. Bake in 350° oven on center rack 30-35 minutes or until toothpick inserted in middle comes out clean and top bounces back when touched.

Serve warm. Top with whipping cream and raspberries.

"Say to the righteous that it shall be well with them,
for they shall eat the fruit of their doings."
Isaiah 3:10

Banana Nut Cake

Ingredients:

1½ cups **GFM's Rice Almond Blend Flour**
1 tsp. baking powder
1 tsp. baking soda
¼ tsp. salt
1 tsp. xanthan gum

½ cup butter
½ cup brown sugar, packed
¾ cup sugar
1 tsp. vanilla
1 cup ripe bananas, mashed
(about 2 medium)
¼ cup buttermilk
4 eggs
1 cup walnuts, chopped

Frosting:
1 ripe banana
¼ cup butter
3 cups confectioners sugar
1-2 Tbsp. milk

GFM Tip:
Sometimes store bought chopped walnuts need to be chopped into smaller pieces.

Directions:

Preheat oven to 350°. Lightly grease and flour two 8 inch cake pans. In a medium bowl add flour, baking powder, baking soda, salt and xanthan gum. Whisk lightly with a fork to combine and set aside.

In a stand mixer cream butter, brown sugar, sugar and vanilla together until light and fluffy. Add banana and buttermilk and mix on low until combined. With mixer on low add one egg at a time until combined. Stop mixer and scrape down sides of bowl. Beat an additional 30 seconds. Add one cup of flour mixture at a time until all flour is combined. Mix an additional 30 seconds. Stir in walnuts. Let sit for 1 minute.

Spread batter evenly into 2 prepared cake pans. Smooth out batter. Bake in preheated 350° oven for 25-30 minutes. Top should be golden brown and will bounce back when touched.

Frosting Directions:
In a mixer bowl combine banana, butter and sugar. Beat on high speed until well mixed. Add milk to thin icing to spreading consistency. If too thin add an extra ½ cup of confectioners sugar.

"Trust in the LORD with all your heart, and lean not on your own understanding;
In all your ways acknowledge Him and He shall direct your paths."
Proverbs 3:5-6

Basic Brownies

Ingredients:

1 cup **GFM's Rice Almond Blend Flour**
⅓ cup unsweetened cocoa
1 tsp. xanthan gum
½ tsp. baking soda
½ tsp. salt
1¼ cup sugar

½ cup butter, melted
3 eggs, slightly beaten
1 tsp. vanilla

chocolate chips or walnuts, optional

GFM Tip:
Line baking pan with waxed paper and lift after baking for easy slicing and transferring to a serving plate.

Directions:

Preheat oven to 350°. Spray 8x8 inch square pan with non-stick cooking spray and set aside.

In a large mixing bowl combine flour, cocoa, xanthan gum, baking soda, salt, and sugar. Whisk until combined. Melt butter in microwaveable bowl covered with waxed paper for 30 seconds. In a small bowl, break eggs and lightly beat with a fork.

Add butter, eggs and vanilla to dry mixture all at once. Mix by hand with a rubber scraper or wooden spoon just until combined. Do not over mix. Pour mixture into prepared pan and spread evenly with rubber scraper. Sprinkle with either chocolate chips or walnuts.

Place in preheated 350° oven on center rack and bake for 30-35 minutes or until toothpick inserted in the center comes out clean. Cool completely.

Yield: 15-20 brownies.

"The LORD is on my side; I will not fear. What can man do to me?"
Psalm 118:6

Chocolate Chip Cake

Ingredients:

1½ cups **GFM's Rice Almond Blend Flour**
2 tsp. baking powder
½ tsp. salt
¾ tsp. xanthan gum

½ cup butter, softened
¾ cup sugar
2 tsp. vanilla
4 egg whites
⅔ cup buttermilk

1 cup mini chocolate chips

GFM Tip:
These cupcakes are a winner for school bake sales or church potlucks.

Directions:

Preheat oven to 325°. Fill muffin pan with muffin cup liners or lightly grease and flour a 12 x 8 cake pan.

In a medium bowl combine flour, baking powder, salt and xanthan gum. Mix lightly with a fork to combine and set aside.

Using a stand mixer cream butter, sugar and vanilla on high speed 2 minutes until light and fluffy. With mixer running on low speed, add one egg white at a time. Scrape down sides of bowl and beat on medium high for 30 seconds. Alternate adding flour and buttermilk until both are mixed into batter. Fold in chocolate chips by hand.

Evenly fill cupcake liners ¼ inch from top of paper or evenly spread batter into cake pan. Bake cupcakes in preheated 325° 18-20 minutes or until top bounces back when touched. Bake cake for 30-35 minutes or until top bounces back when touched and toothpick inserted in center comes out clean.

Frost with chocolate frosting when cool.

*"For God so loved the world that He gave His only begotten Son,
that whoever believes in Him should not perish but have everlasting life."
John 3:16*

Chocolate Pound Cake

Ingredients:

1¾ cups **GFM'S Rice Almond Blend Flour**
2 tsp. baking powder
¼ tsp. salt
1¼ tsp. xanthan gum
½ cup cocoa powder

1 cup butter or margarine, softened
1¼ cups sugar
1 tsp. vanilla
3 Tbsp. milk
5 eggs

GFM Tip:
This recipe will also work with
GFM'S Rice Coconut Blend Flour.

Directions:

Preheat oven to 350°. Grease and lightly flour a 9 inch round cake pan, or a large bread pan for a traditional style loaf.

In a medium bowl combine flour, baking powder, salt, xanthan gum and cocoa powder. Whisk lightly with a fork and set aside.

In a stand mixer, cream butter and sugar until light and fluffy. Add vanilla and milk. With mixer running on low speed add one egg at a time. Stop mixer and scrape down sides of bowl. Turn mixer on medium speed and beat for 1 minute. Slowly add flour mixture until well combined. This batter will look very thick. If batter is too thick for rubber scraper to smooth out top, then add one extra tablespoon of milk.

Spread batter into prepared pan. Evenly smooth out top of batter with a spatula. Bake in preheated 350° oven just below center rack for 45-50 minutes or until toothpick inserted in center all the way to the bottom comes out clean.

If desired drizzle with Chocolate Ganache or serve with fresh raspberries and whipping cream..

* **Refer to the Frostings and Icings section for recipe for Chocolate Ganache.**

"Now the God of hope fill you with all joy and peace in believing, that you may abound in hope, by the power of the Holy Spirit."
Romans 15:13

Chocolate Sour Cream Cake

Ingredients:

1 cup **GFM's Almond Blend Flour**
1 tsp. xanthan gum
½ tsp. baking powder
½ tsp. baking soda
½ tsp. salt

½ cup butter or margarine, room temp.
⅓ cup unsweetened cocoa powder
½ cup sour cream
1 cup unrefined cane sugar
2 tsp. vanilla
3 eggs

½ cup miniature chocolate chips (optional)

GFM Tip: Sprinkle this cake with miniature M & M's before baking instead of using frosting. It makes a great variation and children and adults love the look and taste!

Directions:

Preheat oven to 350°. Grease the bottoms and sides of an 8 x 8 cake pan.

In a medium bowl, combine flour, xanthan gum, baking powder, baking soda and salt. Whisk lightly with a fork and set aside.

If butter is not at room temperature, warm in microwave for 20 seconds. Combine butter, cocoa, sour cream, sugar and vanilla. Beat on medium high speed one minute until well mixed. Add eggs and beat for 30 seconds. Pour half of flour mixture into mixing bowl and stir on low speed for 10 seconds. Repeat with remaining flour. Add chocolate chips to batter and mix until combined. Don't over beat. Mixture should be thick and creamy with all flour absorbed into wet ingredients.

Pour batter into cake pan and smooth top with a spatula. Gently tap sides of cake pan and bottom to release air pockets and level batter.

Place in preheated 350° oven and bake for 30 minutes. If baking cupcakes, reduce baking time to 20 minutes.

"The LORD will give strength to His people; the LORD will bless His people with peace."
Psalm 29:11

Cinnamon Swirl Coffee Cake

Ingredients:

1½ cups **GFM's Rice Almond Blend Flour**
2 tsp. baking powder
1¼ tsp. xanthan gum
½ tsp. salt
3 Tbsp. GF vanilla pudding mix

¼ cup butter, melted
2 tsp. vanilla
¼ cup sugar
2 eggs, lightly beaten
½ cup warm milk (90°-105°)

Topping:
6 Tbsp. butter, melted
2 tsp. cinnamon
¾ cup sugar

GFM Tip:
This recipe will also work well with **GFM's Rice Coconut Blend Flour.**

Directions:

Lightly grease and flour 8 x 8 square cake pan. Preheat oven to 375°. In a medium bowl combine flour, baking powder, xanthan gum, salt and pudding mix. Whisk with fork to combine and set aside.

In a stand mixer bowl add melted butter, vanilla, sugar and eggs. Mix on low speed to combine. Alternate adding flour mixture and warm milk, repeating until gone. Mix on low speed for 30 seconds more to combine.

Melt butter and mix with cinnamon and sugar.

Spread batter evenly into prepared pan. Spread topping evenly across top of cake. With a kitchen knife make a swirl design through top of cake. Use a rubber scraper or spoon and gently move some of topping into the cracks of the swirls.

Bake in preheated 375° oven for 35-40 minutes covering top of cake with foil after 20 minutes to prevent topping from over browning. It is done when toothpick inserted comes out clean. Serve warm.

Serves: 8-12

"I can do all things through Christ, who strengthens me."
Philippians 4:13

Coconut Cake

Ingredients:

1½ cups **GFM's Rice Coconut Blend Flour**
2 tsp. baking powder
½ tsp. salt
1 tsp. xanthan gum

½ cup butter
1¼ cups sugar
2 tsp. vanilla
4 egg whites
¾ cup milk

1 cup shredded coconut

GFM Tip:
This cake also works well with
GFM's Rice Almond Blend Flour.

Directions:

Preheat oven to 350°. Lightly grease and flour a 12 x 8 cake pan.

In a medium bowl combine flour, baking powder, salt and xanthan gum. Mix lightly with a fork to combine and set aside.

Using a stand mixer cream the butter, sugar and vanilla on high speed 2 minutes until light and fluffy. With mixer running on low speed, add one egg white at a time. Scrape down sides of bowl and beat on medium high for 30 seconds. Alternate adding flour and milk until both are mixed into batter. Fold in coconut by hand.

Evenly spread batter into cake pan. Bake cake in preheated 350° oven for 30-35 minutes or until top bounces back when touched and toothpick inserted in center comes out clean.

"Many sorrows shall be to the wicked;
But he who trusts in the LORD, mercy shall surround him."
Psalm 32:10

Fudge Brownies

Ingredients:

1 cup **GFM's Rice Almond Flour Blend**
⅓ cup cocoa
1 tsp. xanthan gum
½ tsp. baking soda
½ tsp. salt
1¼ cup sugar
1 tsp. vanilla

½ cup oil
3 eggs, slightly beaten
⅓ cup Hershey's chocolate syrup
chocolate chips or walnuts, optional

GFM Tip:
For added flavor, dissolve 2 tsp. instant espresso powder into vanilla. This recipe also works well with **GFM's Rice Coconut Flour Blend.**

Directions:

Preheat oven to 350°. Grease 8x8 inch square pan or 12x8 inch pan and set aside. In a large mixing bowl, add flour, cocoa, xanthan gum, baking soda, salt, sugar, and vanilla. Whisk lightly with a fork until combined.

Break eggs into a small bowl and lightly beat with a fork. Add oil and eggs to flour mixture. By hand stir with a rubber scraper or wooden spoon just until combined. Fold in chocolate syrup. Do not over mix.

Pour brownie mixture into prepared pan and spread evenly with rubber scraper. Sprinkle with either chocolate chips or walnuts, if desired. Place in preheated 350° oven and bake for 30-35 minutes or until toothpick comes out clean. Cool completely before cutting.

Note: If brownies rise too much, and you want a more gooey chocolate dessert, take a toothpick just before brownies are done and prick them several times. They will fall to regular size.

*

"Peace I leave with you, My peace I give to you; not as the world gives do I give to you.
Let not your heart be troubled, neither let it be afraid.."
John 14:27

Gingerbread Cake

Ingredients:

2 cups **GFM's Rice Almond Blend Flour**
1¼ tsp. xanthan gum
1 tsp. ginger
2 tsp. baking powder
½ tsp. salt
1 tsp. cinnamon
¼ tsp. cloves

½ cup butter, room temperature
¾ cup molasses
⅔ cup sugar
2 tsp. vanilla
2 eggs
½ cup buttermilk or
(milk with 2 tsp. cider vinegar)
1 tsp. cider vinegar

GFM Tip:
These also work great baked as mini cupcakes. Bake for 15 minutes.

Directions:

Preheat oven to 375°. Lightly grease bottom and sides of an 8x8 cake pan and lightly dust with GF flour. Set aside.

In a medium bowl combine flour, xanthan gum, ginger, baking powder, salt, cinnamon and cloves. Whisk lightly with a fork and set aside.

In a stand mixer beat butter, molasses, sugar and vanilla 1-2 minutes until well mixed. Add eggs, buttermilk and vinegar. Mix on high speed for 1 minute or until well combined. Pour half of flour mixture into wet ingredients and mix on low for 10 seconds. Pour remaining flour and mix on low speed for 30 seconds, or until all flour is mixed in well.

Pour into cake pan and spread evenly with a rubber scraper. Gently tap sides and bottom of pan to release air holes and help gingerbread bake evenly. Bake in preheated 375° oven for 45 minutes or until toothpick inserted in center comes out clean and top bounces back when touched. Cool completely.

Sprinkle with powdered sugar or serve topped with whipped topping .

"For we walk by faith, not by sight."
2 Corinthians 5:7

Old Fashioned Carrot Cake

Ingredients:

2 cups **GFM's Rice Almond Blend Flour**
2 tsp. baking powder
1 tsp. baking soda
1¼ tsp. xanthan gum
½ tsp. salt
1 tsp. cinnamon
¼ tsp. nutmeg
¼ cup golden raisins
¼-½ cup cherry flavored raisins

3 large eggs
½ cup canola oil
½ cup applesauce
2 tsp. vanilla
¾ cup sugar
½ cup brown sugar, packed
2 cups carrots, grated

GFM Tip: Be sure to use a vegetable oil with this cake. Olive oil will make the cake too heavy.

Directions:

Preheat oven to 350°. Lightly grease and flour an 8x8 cake pan.

In a medium bowl combine flour, baking powder, baking soda, xanthan gum, salt, cinnamon, nutmeg and raisins. Mix lightly with a fork to combine and set aside.

Using a stand mixer mix together eggs, canola oil, applesauce and vanilla on low speed for 30 seconds. Add sugar, brown sugar and carrots. Mix for 20 seconds. Remove mixing bowl from mixer. Slowly stir in flour mixture by hand until all the flour is combined.

Evenly spread batter into prepared cake pan. Bake cake on lower rack in preheated 350° oven for 25 minutes and then without removing from oven gently cover with foil. Reduce heat to 300° and bake for an additional 30-35 minutes. Toothpick inserted in center should come out clean and top will lightly bounce back when touched. Allow cake to cool completely. Frost with Cream Cheese Buttercream Frosting.

*** Refer to the Frosting and Icing section for the Cream Cheese Buttercream Frosting recipe.**

"He who believes in Me, as the Scripture has said, out of his heart will flow rivers of living water."
John 7:38

Orange Cupcakes

Ingredients:

1½ cups **GFM's Rice Almond Blend Flour**
1¼ tsp. xanthan gum
2 tsp. baking powder
½ tsp. baking soda
2 tsp. orange zest
¼ tsp. salt

½ cup butter
1 cup sugar
½ cup water
2 Tbsp. orange juice frozen concentrate
1 tsp. vanilla
4 egg whites

GFM Tip:
Before eating oranges, zest the oranges and freeze the zest for future use.

Directions:

Preheat oven to 350° oven . Line cupcake pan with liner cups. In a medium bowl combine flour, xanthan gum, baking powder, baking soda, orange zest and salt. Whisk lightly with a fork until combined. Set aside.

In a stand mixer cream butter and sugar on high speed 2 minutes until light and fluffy. In a liquid measuring cup, measure out water and mix in orange juice concentrate. Pour into mixing bowl, and add vanilla. With mixer running on low speed, add one egg white at time. Beat for 1 minute on medium speed. Pour half of flour mixture into the wet ingredients mixing on lowest speed for 10 seconds. Pour remaining flour into mixing bowl and mix for 30 seconds more on low speed. Pour batter evenly into 12 cup cake liners.

Bake in preheated 350° oven for 20-22 minutes or until tops are lightly browned and toothpick inserted in center comes out clean. Cool completely and then frost with Citrus Icing.

*** Refer to Frostings And Icings section for Citrus Icing recipe.**

"For the kingdom of God is not eating and drinking,
but righteousness and peace and joy in the Holy Spirit."
Romans 14:17

Pumpkin Walnut Cake

Ingredients:

½ cup walnuts, chopped into small pieces

1½ cups **GFM's Almond Blend Flour**
1 Tbsp. baking powder
½ tsp. salt
1½ tsp. xanthan gum
2 tsp. pumpkin pie spice

½ cup butter or margarine
1 cup pumpkin
1 cup sugar
1 tsp. cider vinegar
2 Tbsp. honey
1 tsp. vanilla
3 eggs
½ cup milk (cow, soy, rice, goat)

GFM Tip:
This recipe is great served with a traditional turkey dinner.

Directions:

Preheat oven to 350°. Grease and lightly flour two 8 inch round cake pans. Sprinkle ¼ cup chopped walnuts evenly on the bottom of each pan. Set aside.

In a small bowl combine flour, baking powder, salt, xanthan gum, pumpkin pie spice. Lightly mix with a fork until combined and set aside.

In a stand mixer beat butter, pumpkin, sugar, vinegar, honey and vanilla until light and fluffy. Add eggs and beat for 1 minute on medium speed. Scrape down sides of bowl. Pour in milk. Add half of flour mixture into bowl and mix on low speed for 10-15 seconds. Repeat with remaining flour. Mix on low speed for 30 seconds.

Pour half of batter into each cake pan. Lightly tap the sides and bottom of each pan to level out batter and remove air holes. Bake in preheated 350° oven for 30 minutes or until toothpick inserted in center comes out clean.

Allow cakes to cool completely. Flip one cake out onto cake plate. Frost top of cake with Cream Cheese Buttercream Frosting. Then flip remaining cake out onto top of frosted cake. Frost cake with remaining frosting.

***Refer to Frostings and Icings section for Cream Cheese Buttercream Frosting.**

"Fight the good fight of faith, lay hold on eternal life..."
I Timothy 6:12

Rich Chocolate Truffle Brownies

Ingredients:

1 cup semi-sweet chocolate chips
¾ cup butter or margarine

¾ cup **GFM's Rice Almond Blend Flour**
1 tsp. xanthan gum
½ tsp. baking powder

4 eggs
1¼ cups sugar
2 tsp. vanilla
2 tsp. instant espresso powder

Ganache Frosting:

1 cup chocolate chips
½ cup heavy cream

GFM Tip:
Don't have a double broiler? Place a heat safe bowl on top of a sauce pan filled with 1 inch of water. Bring water to boiling, then reduce heat to low. Add chocolate chips to bowl and melt.

Directions:

Preheat oven to 350°. Grease and lightly flour 8x8 inch square pan. Melt butter and chocolate chips in microwave or double broiler.

In a small bowl combine flour, xanthan gum and baking powder. Mix lightly with a fork. In a large mixing bowl beat eggs and sugar until light and frothy. Dissolve instant espresso in vanilla and add to eggs. Mix well.

Slowly pour melted chocolate into egg mixture, while continually mixing with whisk. Slowly add flour mixture. When all flour is completely mixed in, pour batter evenly into prepared pan. Smooth out top with a rubber scraper.

Bake on center rack of preheated 350° oven 35-40 minutes or until toothpick inserted in middle comes out clean. Allow to cool completely.

For Ganache Frosting: Melt chocolate chips slowly in a double boiler. When melted, remove from heat. Slowly pour cream into mixture and continuously stir until well combined. Pour over top of truffle bars.

"Praise the Lord!...Praise Him for His mighty acts;
Praise Him according to His excellent greatness!"
Psalm 150:1,2

Yellow Cake

Ingredients:

1½ cups **GFM's Rice Almond Blend Flour**
1 tsp. salt
2 tsp. baking powder
½ tsp. baking soda
1¼ tsp. xanthan gum

½ cup butter, room temperature
1 cup sugar
½ cup sour cream
1 Tbsp. vanilla
2 eggs
⅓ cup buttermilk or milk

GFM Tip: If you don't have sour cream use mayonnaise.
For cupcakes bake for 20-22 minutes.

Directions:

Preheat oven to 350°. Grease and flour one 12 x 8 cake pan or two 8 inch rounds. Set aside.

In a medium bowl combine flour, salt, baking powder, baking soda and xanthan gum. Whisk lightly with a fork and set aside.

In a stand mixer, cream butter for about 1 minute until light and fluffy. Add sugar and sour cream and beat for one minute. Add vanilla and eggs. Beat on medium high speed for 1 minute. Scrape down sides of bowl. Pour half of flour mixture into wet ingredients and mix on low speed for 10 seconds. Pour in buttermilk and add remaining flour and mix for 30 seconds. Do not over mix.

Pour batter evenly into cake pans. Smooth out top of loaf with rubber scraper for a good presentation. Gently tap sides and bottoms of cake pan to release air holes and evenly disperse batter.

Bake in preheated 350° oven for 30 minutes or until top springs back when touched and toothpick inserted in center comes out clean.

"...that man should not live by bread alone;
but man lives by every word that proceeds from the mouth of the Lord."
Deuteronomy 8:3

White Cake

Ingredients:

1½ cups **GFM's Rice Almond Blend Flour**
2 tsp. baking powder
½ tsp. salt
¾ tsp. xanthan gum

½ cup butter, softened
1 cup sugar
2 tsp. vanilla
4 egg whites
⅔ cup buttermilk

GFM Tip: Frost with the **Cream Cheese Buttercream Frosting** found in the Frostings and Icings section.

Directions:

Preheat oven to 325°. Fill muffin pan with muffin cup liners or lightly grease and flour a 12 x 8 cake pan.

In a medium bowl combine flour, baking powder, salt and xanthan gum. Mix lightly with a fork to combine and set aside.

Using a stand mixer cream butter, sugar and vanilla on high speed 2 minutes until light and fluffy. With mixer running on low speed, add one egg white at a time. Scrape down sides of bowl and beat on medium high for 30 seconds. Alternate adding flour and buttermilk until both are mixed into batter.

Evenly fill cupcake liners ¼ inch from top of paper or evenly spread batter into cake pan. Bake cupcakes in preheated 325° 18-20 minutes or until top bounces back when touched. Bake cake for 30-35 minutes or until top bounces back when touched and toothpick inserted in center comes out clean.

Frost with your favorite frosting when cooled.

Note: Bake Mini cupcakes for 15 minutes.

"The LORD had done great things for us and we are glad."
Psalm 126:3

Cookies and Bars

"Bless the LORD, O my soul,…
Who satisfies your mouth with good things;
so that your youth is renewed like the eagle's."
Psalm 103:2,5

Cappuccino Chocolate Chip Cookies

Ingredients:

2¼ cups **GFM'S Rice Almond Blend Flour**
¾ tsp. xanthan gum
1 tsp. baking soda
½ tsp. salt

½ cup butter
¼ cup shortening
1¼ cups sugar

2 tsp. vanilla
2 tsp. instant espresso powder
2 eggs

1½ cups chocolate chips

GFM Tip:
For a weaker coffee taste, reduce espresso powder to 1 teaspoon. For stronger taste increase by 1 teaspoon.

Directions:

Preheat oven to 350°. In a medium bowl combine flour, xanthan gum, baking soda and salt. Whisk with a fork and set aside.

In a stand mixer bowl cream butter, shortening, and sugar and on high speed until light and fluffy. In a small bowl dissolve instant espresso powder with vanilla and add to the butter mixture. With mixer on low speed add eggs and mix until combined. Stop mixer and scrape down sides of bowl. Add 1 cup of flour mixture at a time and stir on low speed until all flour is combined. Stir in chocolate chips.

Place rounded tablespoons of dough two inches apart on a cookie sheet. Bake in a preheated 350° oven 10-12 minutes. For a soft and chewy cookie, remove cookies from oven just before tops completely baked. They will finish baking during cooling process. Allow to sit on cookie sheet for 1-2 minutes before removing to a cooling rack.

Yield: 36-40 cookies.

Note: Using a 1 inch cookie scoop works great for perfectly shaped cookies.

"I am the Alpha and the Omega, the Beginning and the End.
I will give of the fountain of the water of life freely to him who thirsts.
Revelation 21:6

Chocolate Chip Pudding Cookies

Ingredients:

2 cups **GFM's Rice Almond Blend Flour**
3 Tbsp. vanilla pudding mix
1 tsp. baking soda
1 tsp. xanthan gum
½ tsp. salt

1 cup butter, softened
¾ cup brown sugar
½ cup sugar
2 tsp. vanilla
2 eggs

1½ cups chocolate chips

GFM Tip:
Use a mixture of white chocolate chips and regular chocolate chips for a change.

Directions:

Preheat oven to 350°. In a medium bowl combine flour, vanilla pudding mix, baking soda, xanthan gum and salt. Whisk with fork and set aside.

In a stand mixing bowl cream butter, brown sugar, sugar and vanilla on high speed until light and fluffy. Stir in eggs. Scrape down sides of bowl. Slowly add flour and mix on low speed until all flour is combined. Do not over beat. Stir in chocolate chips.

Bake in a preheated 350° oven for 10-12 minutes. Remove from oven. Tops of cookies will appear very light brown and almost look as though they aren't done. They will finish baking on the cookie sheet while cooling. After removing from oven allow to remain on cookie sheet for 2 full minutes. (set timer) Remove to cooling racks to finish cooling.

Yield: 36 cookies.

"The LORD Himself goes before you and will be with you; He will never leave you nor forsake you. Do not be afraid; do not be discouraged."
Deuteronomy 31:8

Chocolate Chip Zucchini Cookies

Ingredients:

2⅓ cups **GFM's Rice Almond Blend Flour**
2 tsp. xanthan gum
½ tsp. baking soda
1 tsp. salt
1 tsp. cinnamon

1 cup butter
1 cup brown sugar
½ cup sugar
2 tsp. vanilla
1 cup zucchini, grated
2 eggs
½ cup walnuts
1 cup chocolate chips

Directions:

Heat oven to 350°. In a medium bowl combine flour, xanthan gum, baking soda, salt, and cinnamon. Set aside.

In a stand mixer bowl cream the butter, brown sugar and sugar on high speed until light and fluffy. Add vanilla, zucchini, and eggs. Beat for 30-40 seconds until well combined. Gradually add flour mixture and mix on medium low speed until combined. Add walnuts and chocolate chips stirring on low speed just until combined.

Drop by rounded tablespoon measures onto an ungreased cookie sheet. Bake in preheated 350° oven for 12-14 minutes or until lightly browned for a soft cookie. For a crisper cookie bake 1-2 minutes longer.

GFM Tip:
For perfect grated zucchini use a salad shooter. Cuisinart works great too.

"For the wages of sin is death,
but the gift of God is eternal life in Christ Jesus our Lord."
Romans 6:23

Coconut Oatmeal Cookies

Ingredients:

2 cups **GFM's Rice Coconut Blend Flour**
1 tsp. xanthan gum
1 tsp. baking soda
½ tsp. salt

1 cup butter or margarine
1 cup brown sugar, packed
¾ cup sugar
2 tsp. vanilla
2 eggs

1½ cup certified GF oats
½ cup coconut flakes

GFM Tip:
This recipe also works well with **GFM's Rice Almond Blend Flour.**

Directions:

Preheat oven to 350°. In a medium bowl add flour, xanthan gum, baking soda and salt. Mix lightly with a fork to combine and set aside.

In a stand mixer cream butter, brown sugar, sugar and vanilla on high speed until light and fluffy. Add eggs and mix. Stop mixer and scrape down sides of bowl. Add flour mixture one cup at a time until combined. Fold in oatmeal and coconut flakes, using lowest speed on mixer.

Place rounded tablespoons of dough 2 inches apart on an ungreased cookie sheet. Bake in preheated 350° oven 10-12 minutes, just until middle begins to cook through. Allow to sit on cookie sheet for 3 minutes after removing from oven before transferring to cooling rack.

Yield: 30-36 cookies.

"I am with you always, even to the end of age."
Matthew 28:20

Decadent Chocolate M&M Delights

Ingredients:

1 cup **GFM's Rice Almond Blend Flour**
½ cup unsweetened cocoa powder
¼ tsp baking soda
½ tsp baking powder
1¼ tsp xanthan gum
¼ tsp salt

½ cup butter or margarine
1 cup sugar
1 tsp vanilla
1 egg

1½ cups M&M's

GFM Tip:
If you don't have M&M's, replace with chocolate chips. This recipe is also good with **GFM's Rice Coconut Blend Flour.**

Directions:

Preheat oven to 350°. In medium bowl combine flour, cocoa, baking soda, baking powder, xanthan gum and salt. Mix lightly with a fork to combine.

Cream butter and sugar together on medium speed until soft and fluffy. Add vanilla and egg and beat 30 seconds. Add half of dry mixture and mix on low speed until blended. Add remaining mixture and mix 30 seconds. Scrape sides of bowl to combine all dry ingredients.

Form 1 inch balls and place 2 inches apart on an ungreased cookie sheet. Flatten each ball into ¼ inch thick rounds. Press about 8 M&M's into top of each cookie. Bake in a preheated 350° oven 11-12 minutes. Let cookies remain on cookie sheet for 2 minutes after removing from oven. Transfer cookies to a cooling rack to finish cooling.

Yield: 15-20 cookies

"...for man looks on the outward appearance, but the LORD looks on the heart."
1 Samuel 16:7

Ginger Carrot Zucchini Bars

Ingredients:

1½ cups **GFM's Rice Almond Blend Flour**
¾ cup brown sugar, packed
2 tsp. baking powder
¼ tsp. salt
½ tsp. ground ginger
¼ tsp. orange zest, fresh or dried
1 tsp. xanthan gum
½ cup walnuts, chopped
⅓-½ cup crystallized ginger
(chopped in ¼ inch pieces)

1 cup zucchini, grated
1½ cups carrot, grated
3 eggs
¼ cup honey
½ cup canola oil
2 tsp. vanilla

GFM Tip:
This recipe will also work well with **GFM's Rice Coconut Blend Flour.**

Directions:
Preheat oven to 350°. In a large mixing bowl combine flour, brown sugar, baking powder, salt, ginger, orange rind, xanthan gum, walnuts and crystallized ginger. Set aside.

In a separate mixing bowl combine zucchini, carrots, eggs, honey, canola oil and vanilla. Mix to combine. Pour wet ingredients into dry ingredients and stir by hand just until combined.

Spread batter into ungreased 13x9x2 baking pan and bake in preheated 350° oven on center rack for 30 minutes. A toothpick inserted in center should come out clean. Allow bars to cool completely for 1 hour. Frost with Citrus Icing.

***Refer to Frostings and Icings section for Citrus Icing recipe.**

Yield: 30-36 bars

"And this is the testimony: that God has given us eternal life, and this life is in His Son."
1 John 5:11

Ginger Molasses Cookies

Ingredients:

2 cups **GFM's Rice Almond Blend Flour**
½ tsp salt
1 tsp. soda
1½ tsp. xanthan gum
1 tsp. cinnamon
1 tsp. ground ginger
¼ tsp. ground cloves

¾ cup butter
¾ cup white sugar
¼ cup light brown sugar
2 tsp. vanilla
⅓ cup molasses
1 Tbsp. honey
1 egg

2-3 Tbsp. sugar (for coating)

GFM Tip:
For the best presentation, use an insulated cookie sheet, such as an Airbake.

Directions:

Preheat oven to 350°.

In a medium bowl, combine flour, salt, baking soda, xanthan gum, cinnamon, ginger and cloves. Whisk with a fork to combine and set aside.

In a stand mixer cream butter, sugar, brown sugar and vanilla until light and fluffy. Add molasses and honey to butter mixture. Mix well. Add egg and mix for 30 seconds to combine. Scrape down sides of bowl. Add half of flour mixture to the butter mixture. Beat on low speed just to combine. Repeat with remaining flour. Mix for 30 seconds on low speed or just until flour is combined.

With a ¾ inch scoop or a small kitchen spoon, form dough into ¾ to 1 inch balls. Gently roll in sugar to coat. Place on cookie sheet 2 inches apart. Bake in preheated 350° oven for 10-12 minutes. Allow to sit on cookie sheet for 1 minute before transferring to cooling racks.

Optional: Mix ½ cup confectioners sugar with 1 tablespoon milk. Drizzle in a diagonal motion over tops of cookies for a festive look.

"Cast your burden on the Lord, and He shall sustain you;"
Psalm 55:22

Lemon Bars

Ingredients:

1½ cups **GFM's Rice Almond Blend Flour**
¼ cup powdered sugar
½ cup butter, room temperature
1 Tbsp. cornstarch

3 eggs
1 cup sugar
2 Tbsp. **GFM's Rice Almond Blend Flour**
½ tsp. fresh lemon zest
¼ cup fresh squeezed lemon juice

GFM Tip:
This crust may resemble more of a dough depending on how long you pulse the processor. It still works great.

Directions:

Preheat oven to 350°. Line 8x8 square pan with wax paper and lightly grease.

In a food processor add flour, powdered sugar, butter and cornstarch. Pulse until mixture resembles small pea-sized crumbs or very fine meal. Press dough into prepared 8x8 pan evenly. Bake in preheated 350° oven 15 minutes. Remove from oven.

In a separate bowl whisk together eggs and sugar until frothy. Add flour, lemon zest and lemon juice. Beat well. Pour egg mixture over hot crust. Bake an additional 20-22 minutes or until top just begins to brown lightly. Remove from oven. Cool completely. Sprinkle with powdered sugar.

Carefully lift up wax paper to remove from pan. Cut squares.

Yield: 16-20 squares.

"...He who glories, let him glory in the Lord."
1 Corinthians 1:31

Mochaccino Delights

Ingredients:

2 cups **GFM's Rice Almond Blend Flour**
¾ tsp. salt
¾ tsp. xanthan gum
½ tsp. baking soda

¼ cup butter
⅓ cup cocoa
2 tsp. vanilla
1 Tbsp. instant espresso

¼ cup shortening
¼ cup butter
½ cup brown sugar
¾ cup sugar
2 eggs
1 cup sour cream

1½ cups chocolate chips

GFM Tip: Chocolate glaze with an easy spout for drizzling cookies is now available in grocery stores.

Directions:

Preheat oven to 350°. In a medium bowl add flour, salt, xanthan gum and baking soda. Whisk to combine and set aside.

Using double broiler,* melt ¼ cup butter with cocoa over low heat. While cocoa is melting, in a small bowl dissolve instant espresso with vanilla. After cocoa and butter are melted, remove pan from heat and stir in vanilla and espresso mix.

In a stand mixer bowl beat second ¼ cup butter, shortening, brown sugar and sugar on high speed until softened. Add cocoa mixture to butter/sugar mixture and beat on high speed. With mixer running on low speed add one egg at a time, beating after each. Mix in sour cream. Slowly add one cup flour at a time, until mixed in well. Stir in chocolate chips.

Place rounded tablespoons of batter on an ungreased cookie sheet two inches apart. Bake in preheated 350° oven for 10-12 minutes. Cookies are done if they spring back when touched. Remove from oven and allow to sit on cookie sheet for one minute before removing to cooling rack.

Drizzle Chocolate Glaze or Chocolate Ganache diagonally of over tops of cookies.

*** Refer to Frosting & Icing section for recipe for Chocolate Ganache.**

"The LORD is good, a stronghold in the day of trouble;
And He knows those who trust in Him."
Nahum 1:7

Oatmeal M&M Cookies

Ingredients:

2 cups **GFM's Rice Almond Blend Flour**
1 cup certified GF oats
1 tsp. salt
1 tsp. baking soda
1½ tsp. xanthan gum

1 cup butter or margarine
½ cup sugar
½ cup brown sugar
2 tsp. vanilla
2 eggs
1 Tbsp. honey

2 cups M & M's

GFM Tip:
Don't have M&M's? Use chocolate chips or raisins.

Directions:

Preheat oven to 350°. In a medium size bowl combine flour, oats, salt, baking soda and xanthan gum. Whisk lightly with a fork to combine. Set aside.

Beat butter in a stand mixer until light and fluffy. Add sugar, brown sugar, and vanilla. Beat for 1 minute. Add eggs and honey. Beat for 30 seconds on medium speed.

Add half of flour mixture to wet ingredients. Mix on low speed until partially combined. Repeat with remaining flour. Add M&M's to dough and mix on low speed or fold into dough by hand with a rubber scraper to prevent M&M's from breaking.

Using a one inch cookie scoop, drop dough onto an ungreased cookie sheet 2 inches apart. Bake in preheated 350° oven 12-14 minutes until tops are light golden brown. For a soft chewy cookie be careful not to over bake. After removing from oven, leave on cookie sheet for 2 additional minutes before transferring cookies to cooling rack to finish cooling.

"Ah Lord God! Behold, You have made the heavens and the earth by Your great power and outstretched arm. There is nothing too hard for You."
Jeremiah 32:17

Peanut Butter Blossoms

Ingredients:

1 cup **GFM's Rice Almond Blend Flour**
1 Tbsp. instant dried milk
1 tsp. xanthan gum
⅛ tsp. salt
1½ tsp. baking powder

2 Tbsp. Shortening
3 Tbsp. butter
⅓ cup peanut butter
⅓ cup brown sugar
⅓ cup sugar
1 egg
1½ tsp. vanilla

2 Tbsp. sugar (for coating)
Hershey Kisses

GFM Tip:
This recipe also works great with **GFM's Rice Coconut Blend Flour.**

Directions:

Preheat oven to 350°. In a medium bowl combine flour, dried milk, xanthan gum, salt, and baking powder. Whisk lightly and set aside.

In a stand mixer bowl cream shortening, butter and peanut butter until creamy. Add brown sugar, sugar, egg and vanilla. Beat on medium speed 30 seconds. Add flour mixture all at once and mix on low speed 20 seconds.

Roll 1 inch balls of dough in small bowl of sugar and place on cookie sheet 2 inches apart. Bake in preheat 350° oven for 14-15 minutes. While cookies are baking unwrap Hershey Kisses. Immediately upon removing cookies from oven, place one Hershey Kiss onto center of each cookie, pressing gently. Transfer cookies from cookie sheet to cooling rack to finish cooling.

Yield: 2 dozen.

"For if you forgive men their trespasses,
your heavenly Father will also forgive you."
Matthew 6:14

Peanut Butter Chocolate Cookies

Ingredients:

1¾ cups **GFM's Rice Almond Blend Flour**
⅓ cup unsweetened cocoa powder
1½ tsp. xanthan gum
½ tsp. salt
¼ tsp. baking soda
1 tsp. baking powder

½ cup butter, room temperature
½ cup peanut butter
1¼ cup sugar
2 tsp. vanilla
1 egg

Miniature Reese's Peanut Butter Cup Baking Pieces

GFM Tip:
For an added touch, drizzle chocolate frosting with a zig-zag motion over the tops of these cookies.

Directions:

Preheat oven to 350°. In a medium bowl combine flour, cocoa, xanthan gum, salt, baking soda and baking powder. Whisk lightly with a fork until combined. Set aside.

In stand mixer cream butter and peanut butter on high speed 1 minute until light and fluffy. Add sugar and vanilla and beat 30 seconds longer. Add egg and beat 30 seconds until combined. Add half of flour mixture and mix on low speed 10 seconds. Add remaining flour and mix until combined.

Roll cookie dough into ¾ inch balls and press into ½ inch thick rounds on an ungreased cookie sheet 2 inches apart. Press three or four Reese's Baking Pieces lightly into cookie. Bake in preheated 350 ° oven on center rack for 12 minutes. Allow cookies to remain on cookie sheet for one minute before transferring to cooling racks.

Yield: About 30 cookies

"Behold, how good and how pleasant it is for brethren to dwell together in unity!"
Psalm 133:1

Peanut Butter Cookies

Ingredients:

2 cups **GFM's Rice Almond Blend Flour**
1½ tsp. xanthan gum
½ tsp. salt
¼ tsp. baking soda
1 tsp. baking powder

½ cup butter, room temperature
½ cup peanut butter
1¼ cups sugar
2 tsp. vanilla
1 egg

GFM Tip:
For an added touch, roll in sugar before flattening. Or use chunky peanut butter. This recipe also works well with **GFM's Rice Coconut Blend Flour.**

Directions:

Preheat oven to 350°. In a medium bowl combine flour, xanthan gum, salt, baking soda and baking powder. Whisk lightly with a fork until combined and set aside.

In a stand mixer cream butter and peanut butter on high speed 1 minute until light and fluffy. Add sugar and vanilla and beat for 30 seconds longer. Add egg and beat for 30 seconds. Add half of flour mixture and mix on low speed for 10 seconds. Add remaining flour and mix until combined.

Roll cookie dough into ¾ inch balls and place 2 inches apart on an ungreased cookie sheet. With a fork flatten each cookie with a criss-cross design to ½ inch thickness. Bake for 12 minutes. Remove from oven and allow cookies to remain on cookie sheet for 1-2 minutes before removing to cooling racks.

Yield: 30 cookies.

"...Christ will be magnified in my body, whether by life or by death.
For to me, to live is Christ, and to die is gain."
Philippians 1:20-21

Raisin Jubilees

Ingredients:

2¼ cups **GFM's Rice Almond Blend Flour**
1 tsp. salt
¾ tsp. xanthan gum
½ tsp. baking soda

½ cup butter
¼ cup shortening
1½ cup brown sugar, packed
2 tsp. vanilla
2 eggs
1 cup sour cream

1 cup chopped walnuts
1 cup raisins

GFM Tip:
Try using a mixture of golden and regular raisins for a great flavor.

Directions:

Preheat oven to 350°. In a medium bowl combine flour, salt, xanthan gum, and baking soda. Whisk lightly with a fork to combine and set aside.

In a stand mixer beat butter, shortening, sugar and vanilla until light and fluffy. With mixer running on low speed add one egg at a time until combined. Stop mixer and scrape down sides of bowl. Stir in sour cream. With mixer on low speed add one cup of flour at a time until all flour is combined. Mix on high speed 10 seconds. Stir in walnuts and raisins.

Drop rounded tablespoons of dough two inches apart on an ungreased cookie sheet. Bake in preheated 350° oven 10-12 minutes, or until surface springs back when touched. Cool completely and then frost with Brown Butter Glaze.

*** Refer to the Frostings and Icings section for the recipe for Brown Butter Glaze.**

"He will feed His flock like a shepherd; He will gather the lambs with His arm,
And carry them in His bosom, and gently lead those who are with young."
Isaiah 40:11

Snickerdoodles

Ingredients:

2 cups **GFM's Rice Almond Blend Flour**
1 tsp. baking powder
½ t. salt
1 tsp. xanthan gum

½ cup butter
1 cup sugar
2 tsp. vanilla
2 eggs

2 Tbsp. sugar
1 tsp. cinnamon

GFM Tip: This recipe works well with **GFM's Rice Coconut Blend.** If using this blend add 1 Tbsp. of milk to the batter.

Directions:

In a medium bowl add flour, baking powder, salt and xanthan gum. Whisk lightly with a fork to combine and set aside.

In a stand mixer cream butter, sugar and vanilla on high speed until light and fluffy. Add eggs and mix for 30 seconds on low speed. With mixer running on low speed slowly add flour mixture, one cup at a time, until all flour is combined.

Cover dough with plastic wrap and refrigerate for at least one hour.

Preheat oven to 350°. In a small bowl mix together sugar and cinnamon. With lightly floured hands (GF flour), pinch off enough dough to form one inch balls. Roll dough into one inch balls and then gently roll balls into cinnamon/sugar mixture. Place on cookie sheet 2 inches apart. Bake in preheated 350° for 12-14 minutes. Tops will be slightly brown for a soft, chewy cookie, golden brown for a crispier cookie. Leave on cookie sheet one minute, then remove to or wire cooling rack. Store in airtight container.

Yield: 36-40 cookies

"Therefore the LORD will wait, that He may be gracious to you;
And therefore He will be exalted, that He may have mercy on you.
For the LORD is a God of justice; Blessed are all those who wait for Him."
Isaiah 30:18

Sugar Cookies

Ingredients:

2 cups **GFM's Rice Almond Blend Flour**
1 tsp. baking powder
½ t. salt
1 t. xanthan gum

½ cup butter
1 cup sugar
2 tsp. vanilla
2 eggs

GFM Tip: Instead of using sprinkles frost with the Cream Cheese Buttercream frosting found in the Frostings and Icings section, and then decorate with candy sprinkles.

Directions:

In a medium bowl add flour, baking powder, salt and xanthan gum. Mix lightly to combine and set aside.

In a stand mixer, cream butter, sugar and vanilla until light and fluffy. Add eggs and mix for 30 seconds on low speed. With mixer running on low speed slowly add flour mixture, one cup at a time, until all flour is combined.

Cover dough with plastic wrap and refrigerate for at least one hour.

Preheat oven to 350°. Divide dough into four portions. On a generously floured counter, roll out one portion of dough to ⅛-¼ inch thickness. To prevent rolling pin from sticking to dough lightly dust top of dough with rice flour. Cut out fun shapes with your favorite cookie cutters. Transfer to an ungreased cookie sheet.

Sprinkle with your favorite candy sprinkles, if desired. Place in oven on center rack and bake for 8-10 minutes. Allow to remain on cookie sheet for 1 minute before transferring to cooling racks.

Note: This recipe also works well with **GFM's Rice Coconut Blend Flour**. If using this blend add 1 Tbsp. of milk to the batter.

"...Holy, holy, holy, LORD God Almighty,
Who was and is and is to come!"
Revelation 4:8

Swirled Caramel Toffee Bars

Ingredients:

2¼ cups **GFM's Rice Almond Blend Flour**
1½ tsp. xanthan gum
½ tsp. soda
¼ tsp. salt

1 cup butter, softened
¾ cup brown sugar
½ cup sugar
2 tsp. vanilla
1 egg

1 10 oz. package
Nestle Swirled Caramel Chocolate Chips

Powdered sugar, for sprinkling, optional

GFM Tip: These bars are very rich and taste similar to toffee. This recipe will also work great using **GFM's Rice Coconut Blend Flour.**

Directions:

Preheat oven to 350°. Lightly grease 9x12 inch cake pan. In a medium bowl combine flour, xanthan gum, soda and salt. Whisk with a fork to combine and set aside.

In a stand mixer bowl cream butter, brown sugar, sugar and vanilla 2 minutes until light and fluffy. Add egg and mix 20-30 seconds. Stop mixer and scrape down sides of bowl. Slowly add flour mixture with mixer running on low speed until all flour is combined. Then beat 20-30 seconds longer.

Spread evenly into prepared pan. Bake in preheated 350° oven on center rack for 15-20 minutes. Remove from oven and evenly sprinkle Swirled Caramel Chocolate Chips across top of baked cookie base. Allow to sit 5 minutes, then use a rubber scraper to evenly spread melted caramel and chocolate across top. Allow to cool completely. Lightly sprinkle with powdered sugar, if desired. Cut into 1½ inch bars.

Yield: 36-40 bars

"Let your light shine before men,
that they may see your good works and glorify your Father in heaven."
Matthew:5:16

Triple Chocolate Cookies

Ingredients:

2 cups **GFM's Rice Almond Blend Flour**
1¼ tsp. xanthan gum
3 Tbsp. chocolate pudding mix
⅓ cup cocoa
1 tsp. salt
1 tsp. baking soda

1 cup butter or margarine, room temp.
1 cup sugar
½ cup brown sugar, packed
2 tsp. vanilla
3 Tbsp. Hershey's chocolate syrup
2 eggs

¾ cup white chocolate chips
¾ cup chocolate chips

GFM Tip:
This recipe will also work great with **GFM's Rice Coconut Blend Flour.**

Directions:

Preheat oven to 350°. In a medium bowl combine flour, xanthan gum, chocolate pudding mix, cocoa, salt and baking soda. Whisk lightly with a fork to combine, and set aside.

In a mixer bowl cream butter for 1 minute. Add sugar, brown sugar and vanilla and beat until light and fluffy. Add chocolate syrup and eggs. Beat on low speed just until combined. While mixer is on lowest speed add flour mixture slowly until it is completely combined. Continuing on low speed stir in both white and regular chocolate chips.

With a 1 inch cookie scoop form 1 inch size scoops of dough and place 2 inches apart on a greased cookie sheet. Bake 10-12 minutes in preheated 350° oven, but no longer if you desire a soft cookie. Remove from oven and allow cookies to remain on cookie sheet for 2 minutes. (Set timer.) Remove from cookie sheet and place on cooling rack to cool. Allow cookie sheet to cool an additional 2 minutes more before preparing next batch of cookies to bake.

Yield: 4 dozen

"For all have sinned and fall short of the glory of God,
being justified freely by His grace through the redemption that is in Christ Jesus."
Romans 3:23-24

Ultimate Chocolate Chip Cookies

Ingredients:

2¼ cups **GFM's Rice Almond Blend Flour**
½ tsp. baking soda
¾ tsp. salt
1¼ tsp. xanthan gum

¾ cup butter
¾ cup brown sugar, packed
½ cup sugar
2 eggs
2 Tbsp. honey
2 tsp. vanilla

1½ cups chocolate chips

GFM Tip: This recipe is not meant to be doubled. Also works well with **GFM's Rice Coconut Blend Flour.**

Directions:

Preheat oven to 350°. In a medium bowl combine flour, baking soda, salt and xanthan gum. Whisk lightly with a fork to combine and set aside.

In a stand mixer cream butter, brown sugar and sugar on medium high speed until light and fluffy. Add honey and vanilla and beat for about 10 seconds to combine. Add eggs and mix on medium speed for about 30 seconds.

With mixer running on low speed, slowly add flour mixture until all the flour is mixed in. Mix just until well combined, then add chocolate chips.

Drop rounded tablespoons of dough onto cookie sheet two inches apart. Bake in preheated 350° oven on center rack for 10-12 minutes. Take out just after edges get slightly brown, but center not completely brown for a chewy soft cookie. For a crisper cookie bake until entire cookie is golden brown. Allow cookie to remain on cookie sheet for 1-2 minutes before removing to cooling rack.

Yield: 3 dozen cookies

*"She watches over the ways of her household, and does not eat the bread of idleness.
Her children rise up and call her blessed; her husband also, and he praises her."*
Proverbs 31:27-28

Vanilla Wafers

Ingredients:

1½ cups **GFM's Rice Almond Blend Flour**
1½ tsp. baking powder
¼ tsp. salt
1 tsp. xanthan gum

½ cup butter, room temperature
¾ cup sugar
1 egg
2 Tbsp. honey
1 Tbsp. vanilla

Directions:

Preheat oven to 350°. In a medium bowl combine flour, baking powder, salt and xanthan gum. Whisk lightly with a fork to combine and set aside.

In a mixing bowl cream butter for 1-2 minutes until light and fluffy. Add sugar to butter and mix until combined. Add egg, honey and vanilla. Beat on medium high speed for 30-60 seconds. Stop mixer and scrape down sides of bowl. Pour half of flour mixture into mixing bowl and mix on low speed for 10 seconds. Add remaining flour and beat 20-30 seconds on low speed until well combined.

Lightly flour fingers and hands. Form ¾ -1 inch balls and place on an ungreased cookie sheet 2 inches apart. Bake in preheated 350° oven 10-12 minutes or until tops just begin to brown. Carefully transfer vanilla wafers to cooling rack immediately after removing from oven.

GFM Tip:
Change the flavor to Almond Wafers by reducing vanilla to 2 tsp. and adding 2 tsp. almond flavor.

"And let the peace of God rule in your hearts,
to which also you were called in one body; and be thankful."
Colossians 3:15

Pancakes and Fritters

"Let the word of Christ dwell in you richly in all wisdom, teaching and admonishing one another in psalms and hymns and spiritual songs, singing with grace in your hearts to the LORD. And whatever you do in word or deed, do all in the name of the LORD Jesus, giving thanks to God the Father through Him."
Colossians 3:16,17

Apple Cinnamon Pancakes

Ingredients:

1½ cups **GFM's Rice Almond Blend Flour**
2 tsp. baking powder
¼ tsp. xanthan gum
½ tsp. salt
2 Tbsp. sugar
1 tsp. cinnamon

1 egg, lightly beaten
1 cup milk
2 tsp. canola oil
2 tsp. vanilla
1 squirt of lemon wedge (optional)
1 cup apple, diced

GFM Tip: Dicing an apple: First peel and core apple. Slice ¼ inch wedges. Then turn wedges 90° and slice ¼ inch slices to make perfect ¼ x ½ inch diced apple pieces.

Directions:

In a medium bowl add flour, baking powder, xanthan gum, salt, sugar and cinnamon. Lightly whisk with a fork to combine and set aside.

In a medium bowl lightly whisk egg. Add milk, oil, vanilla and lemon juice to egg and lightly mix together. Add liquid ingredients all at once to the flour mixture. Mix with a whisk to combine. Stir, but do not beat, batter until all the flour is mixed in. Fold in diced apple. Allow batter to rest for 5 minutes.

Heat a skillet to medium high heat. Lightly butter skillet if desired and reduce heat to medium. Drop ¼ cup measure of batter onto hot skillet. Use back of measuring cup to form batter into a circle. Pancake is ready to flip when bubbles start to appear in batter and underside is lightly browned. Flip pancake and cook for 1-2 minutes on other side. If pancake is browning too fast, reduce heat slightly or watch more closely.

Yield: 8-10 thick pancakes.

"...If you shall confess with your mouth the Lord Jesus, and shall believe in your heart that God has raised him from the dead, you shall be saved."
Romans 10:9

Banana Chocolate Chip Pancakes

Ingredients:

1½ cups **GFM's Rice Almond Blend Flour**
2 tsp. baking powder
¼ tsp. xanthan gum
1 Tbsp. sugar
½ tsp. salt

1 egg, slightly beaten
1¼ cups milk
2 tsp. vanilla
2 tsp. canola oil
1 medium ripe banana, mashed (½ cup)
½ cup mini chocolate chips

GFM Tip: To Fold: Cut down through center of batter, along bottom and up side; rotate a quarter turn and repeat.

Directions:

In a medium bowl combine flour, baking powder, xanthan gum, sugar and salt. Mix lightly with a fork to combine.

In a small bowl, lightly beat egg. Add milk, vanilla, and oil to the egg and lightly whisk to combine. Pour wet ingredients all at once into the dry ingredients. Stir by hand to combine. Fold in mashed bananas. Fold in chocolate chips. The batter will be thick. Allow batter to sit for at least 5 minutes. This will help activate the baking powder and allow for more air holes in the finished pancake.

Lightly butter hot skillet and turn heat down to medium. Pour ¼ cup batter onto skillet. Use the back of the measuring cup to spread batter into an even circle. Pancake is ready to flip when bubbles start to appear in the batter and underside is lightly browned. If the pancake is too dark or gets brown to quickly, either reduce the heat or watch more closely.

Yield: 10-12 pancakes.

"The LORD is my strength and my shield;
My heart trusted in Him, and I am helped."
Psalm 28:7

Buttermilk Pancakes

Ingredients:

1 ¼ cups **GFM's Rice Almond Blend Flour**
¼ tsp. xanthan gum
2 tsp. baking powder
1 Tbsp. sugar
½ tsp. salt

2 eggs
2 tsp. vanilla
2 tsp. canola oil
1 fresh lemon wedge (optional)
¾ cup buttermilk

GFM Tip:
Surprise your family by pouring batter into shaped pancake rings.

Directions:

Mix together flour, xanthan gum, baking powder, sugar and salt. Whisk with a fork to combine and set aside. In a separate bowl, break eggs and whisk lightly with a fork. Add vanilla, canola oil and juice from lemon wedge to the eggs.

Make a well in center of dry ingredients. Pour eggs into the well, then pour in buttermilk. Stir together until all flour is mixed in. Batter will be a thick. If too thick, add an extra tablespoon of buttermilk, if too thin add an extra tablespoon of flour.

Preheat skillet over medium heat. Lightly butter skillet if desired Pour batter using a ¼ cup measure onto skillet. Use back of measuring cup to smooth batter into a circle. Pancake is ready to flip when bubbles start to appear in the batter and underside is lightly browned. Flip pancake and finish cooking for 1-2 minutes on other side. If pancake is browning too quickly, reduce heat or watch more closely.

Yield: 8 fluffy pancakes.

"In the beginning was the Word, and the Word was with God, and the Word was God."
John 1:1

Dutch Babies

Ingredients:
(This is a large oven pancake)

¼ cup butter

3 eggs
¾ cup **GFM's Rice Almond Blend Flour**
¾ cup milk
¼ tsp. xanthan gum
2 Tbsp. powdered sugar

GFM Tip:
Did you know that most recipes that are in this cookbook that call for milk can be replaced with a non-dairy alternative such as rice or soy milk?

Directions:

Preheat oven to 400°. Place butter in large glass pie plate or 8 inch glass dish. Place in oven to melt while oven is warming up.

Mix eggs, flour, milk, xanthan gum and powdered sugar in a blender. Blend for 1 minute. Scrape down sides of blender and blend for another 10 seconds. After oven is at 400° and butter is melted, take pan out of oven and pour batter over butter.

Place pan in oven for 20-22 minutes or until edges of pancake are golden brown and center appears cooked through. This pancake puffs up about 2 inches and looks and tastes amazing!

Sprinkle with powdered sugar and serve with syrup or jam.

"Come to Me, all who labor and are heavy laden, and I will give you rest."
Matthew 11:28

Mama's Zucchini Fritters

Ingredients:

3 large eggs
1 Tbsp. milk
1 large clove garlic, (¾ tsp.) minced
¼ cup grated parmesan cheese
½ tsp. salt
¼ tsp. pepper

1½ cups grated zucchini
½ cup **GFM's Rice Almond Blend Flour**
⅛ tsp. xanthan gum

¼ cup olive oil
fresh chopped tomatoes (optional)

GFM Tip:
Can be made dairy free by eliminating parmesan cheese.

Directions:

In a medium glass mixing bowl, break eggs and add milk. Whisk together until slightly blended. Add garlic, parmesan, salt and pepper. Mix well. Add grated zucchini, flour and xanthan gum. Mix well.

Add oil to medium 8-9 inch fry pan and heat on medium heat. Scoop ¼ cup measure of batter into hot oil and flatten with bottom of cup to shape into a circle. Cook 2-3 minutes on each side or until nicely browned. Serve with fresh chopped tomatoes.

Yield: 6-8 fritters

"In the beginning God created the heavens and the earth."
Genesis 1:1

Perfect Crepes

Ingredients:

½ cup **GFM's Rice Almond Blend Flour**
½ tsp. salt
⅛ tsp. xanthan gum
3 Tbsp. margarine, melted
1 cup milk
4 eggs

GFM Tip:
Cooked crepes will keep in a sealed container in refrigerator for up to 3 days. Do not wash crepe pan with detergent. It may give future crepes a soapy taste and also ruin cure. Instead, wipe pan with a paper towel.

Directions:

In a small bowl measure flour, salt and xanthan gum. Whisk lightly. Set aside. Melt margarine in a small glass bowl in microwave 10-15 seconds. Measure out milk.

Add eggs to a blender and blend 10 seconds. Continue blending and slowly add milk; then slowly add flour mixture. Stop blender and scrape down sides. With blender on high slowly add melted margarine. Continue blending 10 additional seconds. Cover with plastic wrap or blender lid and transfer blender container with batter to refrigerator. Allow to rest one hour for a smooth, tender crepe.

Place 1 tablespoon of oil on a non-stick crepe pan and heat 2-3 minutes over medium heat. Wipe out excess oil with paper towel. This cure should be sufficient for entire recipe. When hot, lift pan from heat and pour in enough batter to cover bottom. Batter should make a sizzling sound. Pour excess batter back into blender container, drawing edge of crepe pan across rim. Return to heat and continue cooking 15-30 seconds until surface of crepe looks dull and dry. Turn crepe pan upside down over a storage container, loosen edge with a heat resistant silicone spatula and allow crepe to gently fall out. Bottom of crepe should be slightly browned. Return pan to heat and repeat. You can stack crepe one on top of another.

Yield: 2 dozen thin, tender crepes.

"For I know the thoughts that I think toward you, says the LORD, thoughts of peace and not of evil, to give you a future and a hope."
Jeremiah 29:11

Swedish Pancakes

Ingredients:

4 eggs
3 Tbsp. powdered sugar
1 cup milk

½ tsp. salt
1 cup **GFM's Rice Almond Blend Flour**
¼ tsp. xanthan gum

butter (for skillet)

GFM Tip: I converted this recipe from a very old Copenhagen family recipe that traces back all the way to Sweden.

Directions: 

Add eggs, powdered sugar and milk to a blender and blend for 30 seconds. Add salt, flour and xanthan gum. Blend for an additional 30 seconds.

Heat 10 inch non-stick skillet over medium heat. Butter skillet. Lift pan from burner, pour about ½ cup batter into skillet and spread quickly covering entire pan by tilting from side to side. Cook 1 minute or until underside is golden brown and top appears done. Do not flip over.

With a silicone scraper, fold pancake into thirds and transfer to plate for serving. Sprinkle with powdered sugar and serve with syrup or jam. Repeat by buttering skillet after each pancake.

Yield: 8 pancakes

*"Wisdom is the principal thing; therefore get wisdom.
And in your getting, get understanding."
Proverbs 4:7*

Zucchini Fritters For Two

Ingredients:

2 large eggs
1 Tbsp. milk
1 small clove garlic, (1/2 tsp.) minced
2 Tbsp. grated parmesan cheese
¼ tsp. salt
⅛ tsp. pepper

¾ cup grated zucchini
6 Tbsp. **GFM's Rice Almond Blend Flour**
⅛ tsp. xanthan gum

olive oil (for frying)
fresh chopped tomatoes (optional)

GFM Tip:
This recipe can be fried as one big fritter, then cut in two when done to serve two people.

Directions:

In a medium glass mixing bowl, break eggs and add milk. Whisk together until slightly blended. Add garlic, parmesan, salt and pepper. Mix well. Add grated zucchini, flour and xanthan gum. Mix well.

Add oil to small 8 inch fry pan and heat on medium. Scoop ¼ cup measure of batter into hot oil and flatten with bottom of cup to shape into a circle. Cook 2-3 minutes on each side or until nicely browned. Serve with fresh chopped tomatoes or salsa.

Yield: 2 servings

"God is our refuge and strength, a very present help in trouble."
Psalm 46:1

Crackers, Crusts, Chips and More

"Love suffers long and is kind; love does not envy;
Love does not parade itself, is not puffed up;
Does not behave rudely, does not seek its own,
Is not provoked, thinks no evil;
Does not rejoice in iniquity, but rejoices in truth;
Bears all things, believes all things,
Hopes all things, endures all things."
1 Corinthians 13:4

Almond Blend Chips

Ingredients:

½ cup **GFM's Rice Almond Blend Flour**
¼ tsp. salt
1 Tbsp. vegetable oil
½ cup water
seasoning salt

GFM Tip:
Serve these chips at your next party with your favorite dip!

Directions: 

Preheat oven to 400°. Combine flour and salt in a small bowl and whisk to combine well. Add vegetable oil and work into a fine meal with a fork. Add water and whisk until combined well. Batter will be very thin.

Line a cookie sheet with Non-Stick type Reynolds Wrap Release foil or spray a cold cookie sheet with non-stick cooking spray. Spoon batter by tablespoons onto foil. Spread pools of batter with back of spoon if needed. Stir batter between each tablespoon to prevent ingredients from settling to bottom of bowl.

Bake in preheated 400° oven for 15 minutes until chips are very brown and curled around the edges and centers are slightly lighter golden brown. Remove from oven and sprinkle with plain salt or seasoned salt. Allow to remain on pan for 2 minutes before removing. to wire rack to cool. Repeat with a cool pan for best results.

Yield: About 24 chips.

"For God is not the author of confusion, but of peace…"
1 Corinthians 14:33

Almond Pie Crust

Ingredients:

1 cup **GFM's Rice Almond Blend Flour**
¼ cup almond meal
¼ cup powdered sugar
⅓ cup margarine
⅛ tsp. almond flavor
1 egg white

GFM Tip:
Double all ingredients except egg white for a two crust pie.

Directions:

Preheat oven to 350° . In a medium bowl combine flour, almond meal, and powdered sugar. Place margarine in a small glass bowl and microwave 15 seconds to soften. Blend margarine with a fork until solid pieces are mixed in, then add almond flavor. Pour all at once into flour mixture and work with fork until a mealy dough forms.

Tear two 12 inch squares of waxed paper. Form pie dough into a flattened circle and place on one piece of waxed paper. Cover with second piece of waxed paper and, with a rolling pin, roll out pie dough between sheets of waxed paper into a 10 inch circle ¼ inch thick. Spray straight sided 9 inch pie plate with non-stick cooking spray. Remove top waxed paper from rolled dough and transfer to pie plate. Peal off second sheet of waxed paper. Tears in dough are repaired easily with fingers. Prick pie dough every inch with fork. Separate egg and reserve yolk for filling. Whip egg white with small whisk or fork and brush on bottom and sides of dough with pastry brush. Bake 15 minutes in 350° preheated oven. Let cool completely before filling.

Yield: One 9 inch pie crust.

"Yea, though I walk through the valley of the shadow of death,
I will fear no evil; For you are with me;
Your rod and your staff, they comfort me."
Psalm 23:4

Banana Cream Pie Filling

Ingredients:

¼ cup cornstarch
¼ cup sugar
dash of salt
2 Tbsp. dry milk

2 cups milk
1 egg yolk
1 Tbsp. lemon juice
½ tsp. banana imitation flavoring
2 ripe bananas

GFM Tip: Peel extra ripe bananas, seal in a zip-loc plastic bag and place in the freezer until needed for baking. Thaw slightly and use immediately.

Directions:

In a medium glass bowl combine cornstarch, sugar, salt and dry milk. Mix well. Add milk and egg yolk. Mix well. Add lemon juice slowly while whisking. Mash one banana well and add to mixture with banana imitation flavoring. Mix well.

Microwave filling for 4 minutes, stopping to whisk mixture every minute. Scrape down sides of bowl with a silicone scraper. Microwave 2 minutes more, whisking filling and scraping sides of bowl every 30 seconds until thickened.

Place plastic wrap over bowl of filling and allow to return to room temperature. Whisk frequently. When filling is room temperature, slice second banana into cooled baked Almond Pie Crust. Place slices around outside bottom of crust, then place extra slices in middle area. Pour cooled filling over bananas in pie crust. Cover with plastic wrap and refrigerate until filling is set.

Yield: One 9 inch pie filling.

"For where two or three are gathered together in My name, I am there in the midst of them."
Matthew 18:20

Cheesy Crackers

Ingredients: (Mock Goldfish Crackers)

1 cup **GFM's Rice Almond Blend Flour**
¼ tsp. dried mustard
⅛ tsp. onion powder
¼ tsp. garlic salt
¼ tsp. salt
salt for sprinkling

½ cup butter, room temperature
2 Tbsp. honey
2 tsp. oil
2 cups medium cheddar cheese, loosely packed

GFM Tip: For easy clean up, roll out dough between two pieces of waxed paper. You may need to sprinkle the bottom layer with flour.

Directions:

Preheat oven to 350°. In a small bowl combine flour, dried mustard, onion powder, garlic salt and salt and mix lightly with a fork to combine.

In a stand mixer bowl, combine butter, honey and oil and beat on high speed for 2 minutes until mixture is light and fluffy. Add cheese and mix until combined. Pour flour mixture in all at once. Mix on low speed just to combine, then beat on medium high speed for 3-4 minutes. The dough is completely mixed when it resembles a sugar cookie dough consistency. The cheese will be completely blended into the mixture.

Generously sprinkle countertop with either GFM's Rice Almond Flour Blend or with rice flour. Take a handful of dough and flatten out lightly on floured surface. Sprinkle lightly with flour to prevent rolling pin from sticking, and roll out to ⅛-¼ inch thickness. Cut out with miniature cookie cutters. Place on ungreased cookie sheet and sprinkle lightly with coarse salt if desired.

Place on rack just above center rack. Bake 5-6 minutes in preheated 350° oven. Watch carefully. When edges just begin to turn lightly brown crackers are done. Immediately remove from cookie sheet to cooling racks. Store crackers in an airtight container for up to two weeks.

Yield: 125 one inch crackers.

"Train up a child in the way he should go, and when he is old he will not depart from it."
Proverbs 22:6

Crispy Cinnamon Pie Crust

Ingredients:

¾ cup **GFM's Rice Almond Blend Flour**
¾ cup amaranth flour
¼ tsp. salt
½ tsp. cinnamon
⅛ tsp. nutmeg
1 Tbsp. sugar

¼ cup vegetable oil
⅓ cup milk

1 egg white

GFM Tip:
A straight sided pie plate works best to protect GF crust edges from over browning!

Directions:

Preheat oven to 400° . In a medium bowl combine flour, amaranth flour, salt, cinnamon, nutmeg and sugar. Add oil and work with a fork until a mealy texture forms. Add milk and mix to make dough.

Tear two 12 inch squares of waxed paper. Form pie dough into a flattened circle and place on one piece of waxed paper. Cover with second piece of waxed paper and, with a rolling pin, roll out pie dough between sheets of waxed paper into a 10 inch circle 1/4 inch thick. Spray straight sided 9 inch pie plate with non-stick cooking spray. Remove top waxed paper from rolled dough and transfer to pie plate. Peal off second sheet of waxed paper. Tears in dough are repaired easily with fingers.

Prick pie dough every inch with fork. Separate egg and reserve yolk for filling. Whip egg white with small whisk or fork and brush on bottom and sides of dough with pastry brush. Protect crust edges from over browning with foil or crust protectors.

Option one: Bake 3 minutes in preheated 400° oven. Fill and finish baking according to filling directions.

Option two: Bake pie crust 15 minutes in preheated 400° oven. Remove to a wire rack to cool completely. Fill with unbaked filling.

Yield: One 9 inch crispy brown pie crust.

"If it is possible, as much as depends on you, live peaceably with all men."
Romans 12:18

Lemon Pie Filling

Ingredients:

¼ cup + 1 Tbsp. cornstarch
⅓ cup sugar
2 Tbsp. dry milk
dash of salt
2 cups milk
1 egg yolk
2 drops yellow food coloring
½ cup lemon juice
2 Tbsp. margarine

GFM Tip: This filling tastes great made with the Nutty Pecan Pie Crust.

Directions:

In a medium glass bowl combine cornstarch, sugar, dry milk and salt. Whisk together well. Add milk, egg yolk, and food coloring. Mix well. Add lemon juice slowly while whisking milk mixture vigorously to avoid curdling .

Slice margarine into liquid. Microwave filling for 4 minutes, stopping to whisk mixture every minute. Scrape down sides of bowl with a silicone scrapper. Microwave 2 minutes more, whisking filling and scrapping sides of bowl every 30 seconds until thickened.

Place plastic wrap over bowl of filling and allow to return to room temperature. Whisk frequently. When filling is room temperature pour into cooled baked pie crust. Cover with plastic wrap and refrigerate until filling is set.

Yield: One 9 inch pie filling.

*"Let the words of my mouth and the meditation of my heart
Be acceptable in Your sight,
O LORD, my strength and my Redeemer."
Psalm 19:14*

Nutty Pecan Crust

Ingredients:

1 4 oz. pkg. pecan pieces (1 cup)
½ cup **GFM's Rice Almond Blend Flour**
2 Tbsp. sugar
2 Tbsp. brown sugar
¼ cup margarine

GFM Tip:
Don't have brown sugar? Mix together 1 cup granulated sugar with 1½ tablespoon molasses. Save leftovers in an airtight container.

Directions:
Preheat oven to 350°. Place pecan pieces in a zip-loc bag and crush nuts with a rolling pin until mealy consistency. Empty pecan meal into medium bowl. Add flour, sugar, and brown sugar. Mix with a fork to combine well.

In a small bowl cut margarine into pieces, cover with waxed paper and microwave 15 seconds. Mix margarine with a fork until creamy consistency. Pour into pecan mixture and blend with a fork.

Spray glass 9 inch pie plate with non-stick cooking spray. Empty pecan mixture into pie plate and spread evenly with a fork, working up sides of pie plate and along bottom. Smooth surface with a rubber scraper.

Place in preheated 350° oven for 15 minutes. Remove from oven to a wire rack and let cool completely before filling.

Yield: One 9 inch pie crust.

"Therefore I say to you, whatever things you ask when you pray, believe that you receive them, and you will have them."
Mark 11:24

Rosemary Chips

Ingredients:

½ cup **GFM's Rice Almond Blend Flour**
½ tsp. chicken bouillon
¾ tsp. rosemary needles, crushed
1 Tbsp. vegetable oil
½ cup water
salt

GFM Tip:
Serve with your favorite sour cream dip.

Directions:

Preheat oven to 400°. Combine flour, bouillon and rosemary in a small bowl and whisk to combine well. Add vegetable oil and work into a fine meal with a fork. Add water and whisk until combined well. Batter will be very thin.

Line a cookie sheet with non-stick type Reynolds Wrap Release foil or spray a cold cookie sheet with non-stick cooking spray. Spoon tablespoonfuls of batter onto foil. Spread pools of batter with back of spoon if needed. Stir batter between each tablespoon to prevent ingredients from settling to bottom of bowl.

Bake in preheated 400° oven for 12-15 minutes until chips are brown and curled around the edges and centers are slightly lighter golden brown. Remove from oven and sprinkle with salt. Allow chips to cool on pan for 2 minutes to finish baking centers. Transfer chips to wire rack to cool. Repeat with cool pan for best results.

Yield: 18-24 chips

"It shall come to pass that before they call, I will answer;
and while they are still speaking, I will hear.
Isaiah 65:24

Soft Flour Tortillas

Ingredients:

oil (for skillet)

1¼ cups **GFM's Rice Almond Blend Flour**
1 Tbsp. cornstarch
½ tsp. xanthan gum
1 tsp. baking powder
1 Tbsp. sugar
½ tsp. salt
2 Tbsp. shortening
1 Tbsp. oil
½ cup water

GFM Tip: If you don't have wax paper, lightly dust countertop with flour and roll. Loosen tortilla with a large spatula and place on pan.

Directions:

In a medium bowl combine flour, cornstarch, xanthan gum, baking powder, sugar and salt. Whisk lightly with a fork to combine.

Measure water. Add oil to water. Pour water into flour mixture and add shortening. Mix using a fork until pliable.

Preheat skillet over medium heat. Drizzle about ⅛ teaspoon of oil in pan and spread to coat.

Tear off two sheets of wax paper. Place one piece on the counter and lightly flour. Place a small portion, about 1½ inch ball, onto the wax paper. Set the second sheet of wax paper on top of the dough. Gently roll out dough into a circle shape ⅛ thick. Peel back top portion of wax paper. Pick up wax paper with tortilla up from bottom. Flip over onto skillet, and quickly peel back paper to release. Cook for 30-60 seconds on each side. Transfer tortilla to cooling rack.

Yield: 6-8 tortillas

"...He is my refuge and my fortress;
My God, in Him I will trust."
Psalm 91:2

Soda Crackers

Ingredients:

2 cups **GFM's Rice Almond Blend Flour**
2 tsp. baking powder
½ cup shortening
¾ tsp. xanthan gum
¼ tsp. salt
1 Tbsp. sugar
⅔ cup milk
1 tsp. canola oil

coarse salt (for sprinkling)

GFM Tip: For a different taste sprinkle with grated parmesan cheese.

Directions:

Preheat oven to 375°. Use a non-stick cookie sheet or lightly spray cookie sheet with non-stick spray.

In a mixing bowl add flour, baking powder, shortening, xanthan gum, salt, sugar milk and canola oil. Mix on high speed for one minute.

Divide dough into 3 equal portions. Tear off two large pieces of wax paper. Place on piece of wax paper onto countertop. Lightly dust bottom piece of wax paper with GF flour. Take one portion of dough and form disk in your hand. Place on the wax paper. Place second piece of wax paper on top of dough. Roll out dough with a rolling pin between the wax paper to ⅛ inch thickness. Be sure to roll the dough evenly.

Remove the top layer of wax paper. Take a medal scraper or knife and trim off edges to make a rectangle shape. Carefully pick up the wax paper and flip it over without breaking the dough onto the cookie sheet. Gently peel back the wax paper. Score the dough making even 1½ inch squares. Prick each square 3-4 times with a fork. Sprinkle lightly with coarse salt. Bake in preheated 375° oven just above center rack for 10-12 minutes or until edges just begin to brown. Allow to remain on cookie sheet for 2 minutes before removing to cooling rack.

Optional: Brush with melted butter before removing from cookie sheet.

"The LORD upholds all who fall, and raises up all who are bowed down."
Psalm 145:14

Sour Cream Apple Pie Filling

Ingredients:

1 single GF pie crust
2 cups apples, sliced
1 cup sour cream
¾ cup sugar
1 egg
1 tsp. vanilla
⅛ tsp. salt
2 Tbsp. **GFM's Rice Almond Blend Flour**
½ tsp. nutmeg

Topping:
⅓ cup brown sugar
⅓ cup **GFM's Rice Almond Blend Flour**
1 tsp. cinnamon
2 Tbsp. butter or margarine

GFM Tip: Tastes great with the **Crispy Cinnamon Pie Crust.**

Directions:

Preheat oven to 400°. Peel and slice apples into prepared GF pie crust. Whisk together sour cream, sugar, egg, vanilla, salt, flour, and nutmeg in a medium bowl. Pour evenly over sliced apples.

In a small bowl, combine brown sugar, flour and cinnamon. Cut in margarine and sprinkle evenly over top of pie.

Protect crust edges with foil or crust protectors during baking to prevent over browning. Bake in a preheated 400° oven for 15 minutes. Reduce heat to 350° and bake an additional 30 minutes. Remove from oven to a cooling rack. Allow to cool until filling is set.

"And you will seek Me and find Me,
when you search for Me with all your heart."
Jeremiah 29:13

Sour Cream Onion Chips

Ingredients:

½ cup **GFM's Rice Almond Blend Flour**
¼ tsp. salt
1 tsp. onion powder
2 Tbsp. sour cream
1 Tbsp. vegetable oil
½ cup water
salt

GFM Tip:
Serve with your favorite sour cream dip.

Directions:

Preheat oven to 400°. Combine flour, salt, and onion powder in a small bowl and whisk to combine.

Add vegetable oil and work into a fine meal with a fork. Add sour cream and mix. Add water and whisk until combined well. Batter will be very thin.

Line a cookie sheet with non-stick type Reynolds Wrap Release foil or spray a cold cookie sheet with non-stick cooking spray. Spoon batter by teaspoons onto foil. Spread pools of batter with back of spoon if needed. Stir batter between each teaspoon to prevent ingredients from settling to bottom of bowl.

Bake in preheated 400° oven for 12-13 minutes until chips are brown and curled around edges and centers are slightly lighter golden brown. Remove from oven and sprinkle with plain salt. Let cool on pan for 2 minutes to finish baking centers. Transfer to wire rack to cool. Repeat with a cool pan for best results.

Yield: About 30 small chips.

"Your word is a lamp to my feet and a light to my path."
Psalm 119:105

Thin Crust Pizza

Ingredients:

1 cup warm water (105°-115°)
2½ tsp. yeast
1 Tbsp. sugar

2½ cups **GFM's Rice Almond Blend Flour**
1 tsp. xanthan gum
1 Tbsp. brown sugar
½ tsp. salt
2 tsp. Italian seasoning

1 egg white
1 Tbsp. olive oil
1 Tbsp. honey
1 tsp. red wine vinegar

olive oil (for basting)

GFM Tip: Baste with melted butter and sprinkle with cheese for cheesy breadsticks.

Directions:

Preheat oven to 400°. Lightly spray large pizza pan with non-stick spray.

In a liquid measuring cup stir together warm water, yeast and sugar. Set aside for 5 minutes until foamy.

In a stand mixer bowl combine flour, xanthan gum, brown sugar, salt and Italian seasoning. Stir on low to combine. With mixer on low speed, slowly pour in yeast mixture. Add egg, olive oil, honey and vinegar. Beat on high speed 2 minutes.

Spread dough evenly onto pizza pan. Smooth out top. Cover with a lightweight towel and allow to rest for 15 minutes. Place in preheated 400° oven just above center rack. Bake for 8-10 minutes. Remove from oven.

With a pastry brush, brush olive oil over the entire top of crust. Top with your favorite pizza sauce and toppings. Bake for 10-15 minutes or until cheese is melted.

"Jesus said, Let the little children come to Me,
And do not forbid them; for of such is the kingdom of heaven."
Matthew 19:14

Traditional Pizza Crust

Ingredients:

3 cups **GFM's Rice Almond Blend Flour**
⅓ cup dry milk powder
2 Tbsp. sugar
1 pkg. unflavored gelatin
1 Tbsp. xanthan gum
1½ tsp. pizza seasoning
1 tsp. salt
2½ tsp. rapid rise yeast

4 egg whites
3 Tbsp. vegetable oil
1 tsp. cider vinegar
1⅓ cups very warm water
1 Tbsp. olive oil

GFM Tip: For just one pizza, cool second crust, seal and freeze without topping for future use. To use frozen pizza crust, thaw completely before adding toppings.

Directions:

Preheat oven to 400°. Lightly grease two round 12 inch pizza pans, or solid bottom cookie sheets. Combine flour, powder milk, sugar, gelatin, xanthan gum, pizza seasoning, salt and yeast. Whisk dry ingredients together in a large bowl.

Warm stand mixer bowl under hot water, then dry and put in place. Add egg whites, oil, vinegar, warm water and olive oil to mixer bowl and blend on low speed 30 seconds. Add dry ingredients mixing on low speed. Stop mixer and scrape sides of bowl. Add 1-2 tablespoons of water **only if needed** to make a firm, spreadable dough. Beat dough on high 4 minutes.

Divide dough evenly between two greased pizza pans and spread with scraper into 12 inch circles. Leave outer edges slightly higher and middle an even thickness. Brush crust with olive oil. Bake in preheated 400° oven 12-15 minutes. Top pizza with GF pizza sauce, pizza blend shredded cheese and your favorite toppings. Bake 20-23 minutes more or until topping is melted and crust is crispy.

"The eyes of the LORD are on the righteous,
and His ears are open to their cry."
Psalm 34:15

Vinegar Dill Chips

Ingredients:

½ cup **GFM's Rice Almond Blend Flour**
¼ tsp. salt
1 Tbsp. vegetable oil
½ cup water (- 1 Tbsp.)
1 Tbsp. cider vinegar
1 tsp. dried dill weed
seasoning salt

GFM Tip:
Store chips in airtight container for up to two weeks.

Directions:

Preheat oven to 400°. Combine flour and salt in a small bowl and whisk to combine.

Add vegetable oil and work into a fine meal with a fork. Measure out ½ cup water. Remove 1 tablespoon of water from the measure and replace with 1 tablespoon of cider vinegar. Add vinegar water and whisk until combined well. Add dill weed and stir. Batter will be very thin.

Line a cookie sheet with non-stick type Reynolds Wrap Release foil or spray a cold cookie sheet with non-stick cooking spray. Spoon batter by tablespoons onto foil. Spread pools of batter with back of spoon if needed. Stir batter between each tablespoon to prevent ingredients from settling to the bottom of the bowl.

Bake in 400° preheated oven for 12-15 minutes until chips are brown and curled around the edges and centers are slightly lighter golden brown. Remove from oven and sprinkle with plain salt or seasoning salt. Transfer to wire rack to cool.

"If you abide in Me, and My words abide in you,
you will ask what you desire, and it shall be done for you."
John 15:7

Frostings and Icings

"Are not two sparrows sold for a copper coin?
And not one of them falls to the ground
apart from your Father's will. But the very hairs
of your head are all numbered. Do not fear therefore;
you are of more value than many sparrows.
Matthew 10:29-31

Brown Butter Glaze

Ingredients:

½ cup butter
2 cups confectioners sugar
2 tsp. vanilla
2-4 Tbsp. hot water

Directions:

In a small sauce pan, brown butter over medium heat. Remove from heat and stir in confectioners sugar and vanilla. Continue to stir vigorously. Add 1 tablespoon at a time of hot water until icing reaches spreading consistency.

GFM Tip:
This recipe is meant to be used with the Raisin Jubilees in the Cookies and Bars section.

"Sing to the LORD a new song,
And His praise in the assembly of saints."
Psalm 149:1

Chocolate Frosting

Ingredients:

½ cup chocolate chips
3 Tbsp. butter
2 Tbsp. shortening

1½ cups powdered sugar, sifted
2 Tbsp. corn syrup

2-3 Tbsp. hot water, as needed

GFM Tip: Slowly add hot water continuing to stir to keep chocolate from becoming lumpy.

Directions:

Using a double boiler, slowly melt chocolate chips, butter and shortening. Remove from heat and stir in powdered sugar and corn syrup. Continue mixing well. Add 2-3 Tbsp. of hot water as needed to desired spreading consistency.

Frost cake immediately.

"Put on the whole armor of God,
That you may be able to stand against the wiles of the devil."
Ephesians 6:11

Chocolate Ganache

Ingredients:

1 cup semi-sweet chocolate chips
½ cup heavy cream

2 tsp. corn syrup (optional)

Directions:

Slowly melt chocolate chips in a double broiler. Remove from heat. Slowly pour cream into melted chocolate while whisking constantly.

For a shiny Ganache, stir in two teaspoons of corn syrup.

Yield: Frosting to cover 1 single layer cake or brownies.

GFM Tip:
For a coffee flavor dissolve 1 Tbsp. of instant espresso into heavy cream.

"The LORD is my rock, and my fortress and my deliverer;
My God, my strength, in whom I trust."
Psalm 18:1

Citrus Frosting

Ingredients:

8 oz cream cheese
½ cup sifted powdered sugar
2 Tbsp. orange juice concentrate
1 Tbsp. orange zest, fresh
or 2 tsp. dried orange zest

GFM Tip:
Make this frosting lemon flavored by replacing orange juice concentrate with 2 Tbsp. fresh squeezed lemon and 1 tsp. fresh lemon zest.

Directions:

In a stand mixer beat cream cheese for 1 minute until soft. Add powdered sugar, orange juice concentrate and orange zest. Beat for 2 minutes until light and fluffy.

"Bless those who persecute you; bless and do not curse."
2 Timothy 3:12

Cream Cheese Icing

Ingredients:

4 oz. cream cheese, room temperature
3 Tbsp. butter
¾ cup powdered sugar
½ tsp. vanilla
1 Tbsp. milk

GFM Tip: This frosting is great on the Cinnamon Rolls found in the Rolls and Biscuits section.

Directions:

In a stand mixer, beat cream cheese, butter, powdered sugar, vanilla and milk until all ingredients are mixed in well.

Add extra milk 1 Tablespoon at a time until the desired spreading consistency is reached.

"Jesus said… 'I am the Way and the Truth and the Life; no one comes to the Father except through Me."
John 14:6

Cream Cheese Buttercream Frosting

Ingredients:

½ cup shortening
½ cup butter
4 oz cream cheese, softened
2 tsp. vanilla

4 cups GF powdered sugar, sifted
1-2 Tbsp. milk (if needed)

Food coloring (optional)

Directions:

Beat shortening, butter and cream cheese together 3 minutes on high speed. Add vanilla and mix.

With mixer on low speed, slowly add powdered sugar, ½ cup at a time, until reaching desired consistency. If needed, add 1 tablespoon milk at a time to thin frosting to spreading consistency.

Add food coloring if desired and frost cookies, cakes, and cupcakes to your delight!

GFM Tip:
Try adding flavors such as strawberry, orange, almond, and mint in place of the vanilla for a flavored icing.

"The LORD God is my strength; He will make my feet like deer's feet,
And He will make me walk on my high hills."
Habakkuk 3:19

We hope that you enjoyed our cookbook.

"Let not your heart be troubled;
You believe in God, believe also in Me.
In My Fathers house are many mansions;
If it were not so, I would have told you.
I go to prepare a place for you.
And if I go and prepare a place for you,
I will come again and receive you to Myself;
that where I am, There you may be also. "
John 14:1-3

A TESTIMONY OF FAITH AND HEALING

After a three-day stay in the hospital for corrective surgery, I experienced a very itchy red rash for months that affected the shins, tailbone, under breasts, forearms and neck. After trying many things, a friend who has Celiac Sprue suggested eating a gluten free diet. She had experienced the same type of rash in the same areas of her body that she called Dermatitis Herpetiformis, a skin rash associated with Celiac Sprue. The Merck manual says this autoimmune disease causes clusters of intensely itchy blisters and hive like swellings that have nothing to do with the herpes virus but instead, gluten proteins in wheat, barley and rye products cause the rash and itching in the skin.

I decided to experiment by going on a gluten free diet to see if it helped. I knew it might take some time before I might see improvement. In fact, some information claimed the rash does not go away without a strict gluten free diet plus medication. Eating a gluten free diet was a bit difficult because I started between Thanksgiving and Christmas. However, I began to see improvement after about one month.

Then my daughter broke both her wrists in a car accident and I went to help out for an extended time. Because she lives in a very remote area, traveling two hours every other week to get groceries was the usual pattern. Cooking for a family of five and still maintaining a gluten free diet became impossible in this situation and the rash soon became intense again.

I had been praying and believing God's Word concerning healing and one night during my evening devotions I knew in my spirit I was healed. The rash was still there and itching continued but I knew beyond a doubt I had received my healing based on God's Word and not what I could see or feel. I had made a faith connection. From that point on the rash gradually began to improve until one month later it was completely gone! All Praise to God!

My healing did not just happen. I had to build my faith before I could believe. S o how did I build my faith? I dug into the Word. *"So then Faith comes by hearing, and hearing by the Word of God.*" (Romans 10:17) I noticed that faith comes by hearing and hearing… that means I needed to have the Word of God dwelling in me continually.
To build my Faith I needed to know and believe it ***is*** God's will to heal me. But how do I know what God's will is? Some people may think it is not God's will to heal them, but I could not find any scripture to support that idea. In fact, I found the opposite. In Matthew 9:20-22 it says, *"For she kept saying to herself, if I only touch His garment, I shall be restored to health. Jesus turned around and, seeing her, He said, Take courage daughter! Your faith has made you well."* I learned that out of the 19 people healed in the Gospel accounts, that Faith is specifically mentioned in 12 accounts. In the Luke 8:46 account Jesus did not even know the woman who touched his garment was there until healing power (virtue) was gone out of Him. I was learning that healing power is in His very Being and I needed that faith connection.

A TESTIMONY OF FAITH AND HEALING

Some people may think that God is trying to teach them something through their sickness, but I could find no scripture to support that idea either. Scripture says he uses the Word, not sickness, to teach us. *"All scripture is given by inspiration of God, and is profitable for doctrine, for reproof, for correction, for instruction in righteousness;* " 2 Timothy 3:16. I was learning that what I believed must be supported by scripture, and based God's Word alone.

So, I went to the Word to see what it said. John 10:10 says, *"The thief comes not, but to steal, and to kill, and to destroy: I am come that they might have life, and that they might have it more abundantly."* So Satan is the destroyer and Jesus is the healer. I decided never to attribute to God or to blame God for the works of the enemy. Luke 13:16 states, *"And ought not his woman, being a daughter of Abraham, whom Satan hath bound, lo, these eighteen years, be loosed from this bond on the Sabbath day?"* Jesus also demonstrated his compassion and desire to heal **all** who were oppressed of the devil. "*How God anointed, Jesus of Nazareth with the Holy Ghost and with power: who went about doing good, and healing all that were oppressed of the devil; for God was with him.*" Acts 10:38. *"...and great multitudes followed him, and he healed them all;"* Matt. 12:15 (Also see Luke 6:19) So if Jesus healed them all, and "*He is the same yesterday, today and forever.*" Hebrews 13:8, and he changes not, *"I am the Lord, I change not;"* Malachi 3:6, and *"...there is no respect of persons with God,"* Romans 2:11, therefore if it was His will to heal them, then it is His will to heal me also.

I learned that one of the Redemptive Names of God was Jehovah Rapha, meaning 'for I am the Lord who heals you'. It is in His Being. It's who He is! The Great Physician.

I found that healing and salvation were in the same package, even in the same verse. Isaiah 53:4-5 (Amplified) says, "*Surely He has borne our griefs (sicknesses, weaknesses, and distresses) and carried our sorrows and pains (or punishment), yet we (ignorantly) considered Him stricken, smitten, and afflicted by God (as if with leprosy). But He was wounded for our transgressions, He was bruised for our guilt and iniquities; the chastisement (needful to obtain) peace and well-being for us was upon Him, and with the stripes (that wounded) Him we are healed and made whole."* And Matthew 8:17, "*And thus He fulfilled what was spoken by the prophet Isaiah, He Himself took (in order to carry away) our weaknesses and infirmities and bore away our diseases."* 1 Peter 2:24 states, *"Who his own self bare our sins in his own body on the tree, that we, being dead to sins, should live unto righteousness; by whose stripes ye* ***were*** *healed."* I noticed it was past tense. So healing is available to me and it has already been bought and paid for by my Lord. How do I receive it?

A TESTIMONY OF FAITH AND HEALING

I remembered a speaker stating that healing was not physical but spiritual. And I remember thinking, 'Not physical? I sure thought it was!' Now I began to understand. It was done, past tense in the spirit. I just needed to receive what the Lord had already done. I have heard it said that the reason we may not be healed is because we don't have enough faith. I learned from Romans 12:3 that *"God has dealt to each one a measure of faith."* Every born again Christian has that measure of faith. I just needed to develop my faith. I needed to make that faith connection for Hebrews 11:1,6 states without faith it is impossible to please Him. *"Now faith is the substance of things hoped for, the evidence of things not seen. But without faith it is impossible to please Him, for he who comes to God must believe that He is, and that He is a rewarder of those who diligently seek him."* I knew I had to dig in.

I began to diligently seek Him. James 5:15-16 says, *"And the prayer of faith shall save the sick, and the Lord shall raise him up; and if ye have committed sins, they shall be forgiven him. Confess your faults one to another, and pray one for another, that ye may be healed. The effectual fervent prayer of a righteous man avails much."*

I had made my faith connection and I knew *"..it is God which works in you both to will and to do of His good pleasure,"* Philippians 2:13. I had heard people say that you never know what God might do but I found that it is not a mystery. He tell us in his Word what he will do. It is God *"Who forgives all your iniquities, who heals all your diseases."* Psalm 103:3.

In the process of searching out God's Word I also learned there are things that can block our receiving the healing that God has already provided, such as unforgiveness (Matthew 6:14), doubt (James1:5-8), unbelief (Matthew 13:58 & Mark 6:5-6), and fear (Job 3:25). And we must also operate in the law of love, (Matthew 22:37-40).

Billie McCrea

Scriptures in this testimony were taken from the King James Version - Amplified Version Parallel Bible, Zondervan Publishing House, Grand Rapids, MI, or New King James Version God's Word for Every Circumstance, Revised Edition, published by Christian Faith Center, PO Box 98800, Seattle, WA 98198. I love the Amplified version because it includes the original Hebrew and Greek meaning of words often lost in the English translations.

ABOUT THE AUTHORS

Rachel Carlyle-Gauthier is the mother of three beautiful daughters, a wife and business owner. She and her family live in the mountains of the Mission Valley of Montana. Rachel's passion for cooking began in high school, cooking for 200 students three times a day while attending private school in Louisiana. She later attended the Bon Vivant School of Cooking in Seattle, Washington, earning certificates in Mastering the Basics, Art of Fine Cuisine, Cordon Bleu and the Art of Baking Bread. After nine years of dedicated motherhood and committed service in women's ministries at her local church, Rachel is excited about the new endeavor the Lord is inspiring her in and prays that each person using Gluten Free Mama products will be blessed and positively impacted.

Billie McCrea grew up on a ranch in western Montana and helped cook for farm hands at an early age. The family raised a garden so canning and freezing were part of the harvest experience. It only seemed natural that Home Economics would become a life vocation which she combined with a teaching degree and Art while attending the University of Montana. Billie's hobbies include watercolor, tole painting, rubber stamping, sewing and cooking. Billie and her husband have been married 45 years and share a strong relationship with the Lord. They have led home Bible Study groups for over 25 years. Billie also serves the Lord as a prayer room worker for her church. She and her husband have two grown children and three grandchildren.

REFERENCES

The Food Allergy & Anaphylaxis Network. (2005). Tips For Managing an Egg Allergy. **Retrieved January 15, 2007, from www.foodallergy.org/allergens/egg.html.**

Recipezaar. (2007). Egg Substitutes. **Retrieved January 8, 2007, from www.recipezaar.com/library/getentry.zsp?id=424**

Wholesome Sweeteners. (2004). Wholesome Sweeteners Fair Trade Natural Cane Sugar. **Retrieved February 22, 2004, from http://www.wholesomesweeteners.com/brands/wholesome Wholesome_Sweeteners_Fair_Trade_Natural_Cane_Sugar.html**

Wholesome Sweeteners. (2004). Wholesome Sweeteners Fair Trade Turbinado Sugar. **Retrieved February 22, 2004, from http://www.wholesomesweeteners.com/brands/wholesome/Wholesome_Sweeteners_Organic_Turbinado_Sugar.html**

The Bee Guys. (2004). Old North State Apiaries, Helpful Hints. **Retrieved February 22, 2004, from http://beeguys.com/recipes.html**

INDEX

INDEX

INDEX

Printed in the United States
213650BV00002B/2/A

9 781602 664098